Roger Pulvers is an author, playwright, theater director, translator and filmmaker. He has published more than fifty books in Japanese and English, including novels, essays, plays and poetry. Working as assistant to director Oshima Nagisa on *Merry Christmas, Mr. Lawrence* brought him back to Japan and inspired him to become the award-winning playwright, film director and prolific author he is today. His novel, *Hoshizuna Monogatari* (*Star Sand*), which he wrote in Japanese, was published by Kodansha, Japan's largest publisher, in 2015, and subsequently in English and French in 2016 and 2017 respectively. It was released as a film, directed by him, in 2017. His most recent books are the novels, *Half of Each Other* and *Peaceful Circumstances*, his autobiography, *The Unmaking of an American*, and a cultural memoir, *My Japan*, all published by Balestier Press.

ALSO BY ROGER PULVERS

Liv

Half of Each Other

The Honey and the Fires

The Dream of Lafcadio Hearn

Peaceful Circumstances

The Unmaking of an American

My Japan

The Charter—and Thirteen Other Stories about Japan

TRANSLATIONS

Night on the Milky Way Train and Nine Other Stories
by Kenji Miyazawa

The Illusions of Self: Tanka by Takuboku Ishikawa

WHOLLY ESENIN

Poems by SERGEI ESENIN

Translation from the Russian, Notes and Commentary by

ROGER PULVERS

BALESTIER PRESS
LONDON · SINGAPORE

Balestier Press
Centurion House, London TW18 4AX
www.balestier.com

Wholly Esenin: Poems by Sergei Esenin
Translations from the Russian, Notes and Commentary

A CIP catalogue record for this book
is available from the British Library.

ISBN 978 1 911221 91 3

Cover illustration by Alice Pulvers

This book is dedicated to the memory of my three remarkable and impassioned professors of Russian. Vladimir Fyodorovich Markov (1920-2013), world expert on Russian formalism, my first teacher of Russian conversation at UCLA in 1961; Kiril Fyodorovich Taranovsky (1911-1993), whose seminars on Russian poetry at Harvard Graduate School in 1964 were breathtakingly profound; and Roman Osipovich Jakobson (1896-1982)—his seminar on Russian prosody, also at Harvard in 1965, opened up the world of lyricism and symbolism in poetry to me. Without their inspiration, which has not diminished in magnitude for a day since those times, this book would never have been written or seen the light of day. My dear and wonderful professors, thank you for a lifetime of adventure and enlightenment!

CONTENTS

Introduction

Sergei Esenin is the Dylan Thomas of Russia, only much prettier. Both were poets who extolled the nature and mores of their native regions—for Thomas, the area around Swansea in Wales; for Esenin, his birthplace in the Russian countryside in the vicinity of the ancient city of Ryazan. The use of the speech rhythms and tonality of their home districts, frequent archaic language and some neologisms is another common feature of their poetry. What they particularly had in common, however, was an indestructible nostalgia for their childhood homes and the tendency to be happier when they were away from them. Both loved women but were not particularly successful at pleasing them; both had curly light-colored hair; and both ended their lives unable to tread in a sea of alcohol. Dylan Thomas, who lived some nine years longer than Esenin, read his poetry beautifully. Esenin did too. Their publics adored them.

Sergei Esenin—whose name might rightfully be transliterated beginning with a Y, for it is pronounced Ye-SAY-nin—has been, since his death in 1925, Russia's most popular modern poet, and this in a country where poetry itself is nearly as popular as music.

There is a vast body of writing dedicated to his poetry. Some of it is not uncritical. Especially during his lifetime he copped it from both sides of the ideological fence. To many diehard ideologues he was simply out of step with the "new" Russia: Neither the honesty nor sheer beauty of his lyrics could amount to a hill of beans when compared to the monumental, glorious and lofty future that communism was going to afford the many nations of people that comprised the Union of Soviet Socialist Republics. On the other hand, to many avant-garde poets and literati of his day, Esenin was not only the last poet of the village, as he described himself, but the ultimate poseur of all rural Russia, gallivanting around Moscow in his snow-white *rubashka*, or traditional Russian shirt, and playing the provincial rake as he mowed through rows of swooning city girls who couldn't get enough of him, the sight of his gorgeous golden hair or the touch of his gorgeous flowing lyrics.

The great poet Anna Akhmatova was sceptical of his gift, though she admitted late in life that she was perhaps put off by his obsession with rusticity; and D.S. Mirsky, the eminent literary historian, considered his entire work a very mixed bag. Those who lost themselves in his poetry were looked down upon by some as, at best, readers of unsophisticated taste and, at worst, sentimental hicks.

His messages are, indeed, mixed. He is on again off again when it comes to almost everything, including his motherland, his women, even the home district that he waxed so passionately about most of the time. Like many of his compatriots, he both highly praised and vilified American life, which he saw at first hand when he went there with his wife, the dancer Isadora Duncan. He admired America's industrial achievements, something his economically backward country could only ogle from afar. But he failed to see anything of cultural value in the United States, believing that the only thing Americans truly loved was *biznes*. He saw little art and no poetry in American life. But then again, how could he, with his smattering of English and his self-centered, if ever wounded, pride as the native son of the new world empire of people's democracy?

Yet the thing Esenin is most contradictory about is himself. Sergei Esenin is an open book that all can readily access; and for this we should be grateful. Few poets are as brutally honest with themselves as he is. It is this honesty that we are attracted to today, an honesty that puts everything from his teenage caprices to his stark adult sins under the magnifying glass of poetic expression.

The ideologues of the Soviet state fought hard to extinguish his memory. For quite a long time after his death, anyone revering him in print was censured. Even in the postwar years, a Soviet citizen caught "proselytizing" youth by distributing Esenin's poetry was eligible for a hefty prison sentence. *Khuliganstvo* (see note on page 65) was—and still is—a crime in Esenin's homeland. And here he was, as he still stands today: the father—and now granddaddy—of all the hooligans.

Now there are nearly two dozen monuments to and busts of Esenin in his country. The government has issued stamps in his honor, as well as a two-ruble silver coin to mark, in 1995, the centenary of his birth. There are scores of songs sung by individual singers as well as choral works with his poems as lyrics. The fact that his poetry lends itself so exquisitely to music may be one of the best proofs of its lasting beauty. A café restaurant called "Esenin" opened in Moscow in October 2015 at No. 8 Novaya Ploshchad (New Square), "designed in the style of the Silver Age (see page 17) ... where the master chef creates his culinary masterpieces like a poem." But photographs of café-restaurant Esenin's interior reveal deep purple sofa-like seating and a large light fixture reminiscent less of the Silver Age than of a gigantic brass slinky dangling from the ceiling. Perhaps these features might indeed have convinced the poet himself that he was definitely in the grips of one of his slurred alcoholic stupors.

If Esenin's poetic Russia did not reflect the reality of his country between 1917 and the fall of the communist regime in 1991, it has a good deal in common with the reality—for better and worse—of his country today, with its intense religious influence on mores and social policy and its idealization of "Russian values."

Were he alive today, Sergei Esenin would at least recognize Russia, something that he was largely unable to do during the last years of his life.

Roger Pulvers
2020

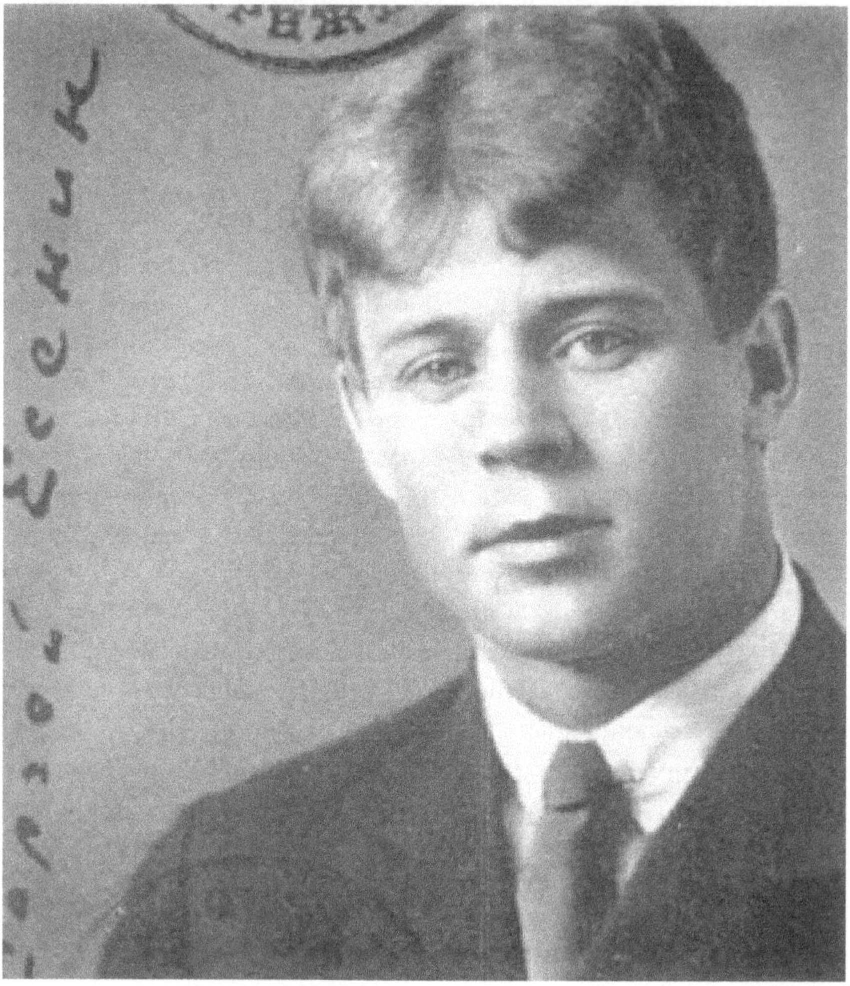

PART ONE

The Early Years

"I feel a heavy, hopeless sadness!" he wrote in July 1912, not long after arriving in Moscow, to a friend back home. "I don't know what to do with myself. Suppress all feelings? ... Why go on living, a useless weak and blind worm?"

In hindsight, perhaps prophetic words. But at the time, those of a moody teenager who misses home. In fact, the letter is full of paraphrases of a popular song and other, more literary, references.

Poor young Sergei ... he had gone, barely seventeen, to Moscow to live with his father, with whom he had spent almost no time in his childhood. His father was working as a clerk-cum-salesman in a large butcher shop. If he suffered from intense feelings of homesickness and an even more intense ambition to become a recognized poet, what else could one expect from a lonely teenage boy except a crushing hopeless sadness?

His home life as a child had been far from ideal. His mother and father lived apart almost from the beginning of their marriage, though he refused to grant her a divorce. According to one of his sisters, Sergei considered himself an orphan, and he suffered from being offended even more than an actual orphan. Their mother, probably enduring a similar kind of depression that he experienced in later life, drank heavily and beat her children.

Reading the poem he wrote as a letter to his mother (see page 140), you would naturally think that he longed for his mother and the affection she showed him. But when he wrote this poem his mother was only forty-nine, not the *starushka*, or old woman, he refers to. He may as well have titled it "A Letter to my Grandmother." Esenin is not writing about his mother but about the icon of Mother; as when he waxes over his village and his Russia, he is creating an icon of Village and Old Russia. In one of his last poems he wrote: "I am like a foreigner in my own land." In fact, by the end of his life he was estranged not only from his land but from his elders, his village and his era.

Esenin's early letters give the portrait of a diffident, insecure and highly moody boy. But this type of insecurity was tied—as it often is in teenagers—with a burning ambition to "be somebody." He had the chutzpah to write to Alexander Blok, the foremost poet of his time and an immensely popular figure in all of Russia (on 9 March 1915) ...

I would like to speak with you. The matter is very important to me. You don't know me, but maybe you've come across my name in journals. I'd like to visit you around 4.

With respect
S. Esenin

That's the entire letter. He had gone to St. Petersburg (renamed Petrograd to avoid the Germanic association of Russia's enemy at the time) specifically to meet Blok. He had no idea how to contact the famous poet and, apparently, ended up asking in a big bookstore if anyone knew where he lived. Luckily enough, one of the staff did. When he eventually showed up at Blok's home, the elder poet welcomed him, recommending for publication some of his poems, which he found "fresh, pure (and) sonorous ... if wordy...."

Esenin was awed by Blok, breaking out in a profuse sweat because "he was the first living poet I ever laid eyes on." He went on to meet many poets in what was then the nation's capital. The city was crawling with poets. You could find one wherever there was a foggy lamppost to stand under. He returned to Moscow with a much inflated ego, and his wife Anna felt that he was "already someone else."

Yet, despite his complexes—as a perceived country bumpkin, a perception that he played upon later to great effect; and as a vociferous medium for the fast-disappearing old Russia—he was affable and most sociable as he moved within a wide sphere of friends and acquaintances, many of them much older famous artists, authors, critics and publishers.

Perhaps it is an exaggeration to say that this wonder boy of the outback, this supremely charismatic voice of the old—hence "real"—Russia had taken Moscow and St. Petersburg by storm. Nevertheless, it can be said that, in the span of a few years, he became a star in those cities, one whose light could be shunned but not ignored.

Sergei Esenin was born on 3 October 1895 in Konstantinovo, a village overlooking the Oka River, some forty-three kilometers from the city of Ryazan. Ryazan itself is about two hundred kilometers southeast of Moscow. Settled around the year 800, the city is more than three hundred years older than Moscow. Esenin died in St. Petersburg on 28 December 1925, aged thirty. His father outlived him by five years; his mother, by nearly thirty. His elder sister Ekaterina died in 1977; his younger sister, Alexandra, in 1981.

For the first three years of his life he lived with his paternal grandmother before moving to the home of his maternal grandfather. He lived there from 1899 to 1904. This grandfather, with his strong faith, had a major impact on Esenin's orientation toward religious imagery in his poetry.

But Esenin's religious upbringing did not produce the kind of believer that the people of Konstantinovo recognized. He wrote from Moscow to his best friend Grisha Panfilov in November 1912 that he did not believe in the way that others believe. He told Grisha that their belief originated in fear of death, while his stemmed from faith in a Christ gifted "with a lucid mind and a noble spirit," and that these provided a model for posterity to love all human beings.

(Grisha Panfilov's death, from tuberculosis on 25 February 1914, shook Esenin to his core; and the grief remained with him until the end of his own life.)

From an early age, then, he was out of step with Russia's faith, Russian Orthodoxy.

"Grandpa considered me an atheist," he wrote years later, "and crossed himself whenever he saw me. Like when, on a lark, I broke off a piece of a wooden icon in the house to light the samovar. What an uproar that caused! My whole family just about damned me to hell for that!"

In 1909, when he turned fourteen, he began attending the Spas-Klepiki school, where he studied to be a teacher and remained for three years. But he came to the conclusion that a teaching career was not for him. Even in his mid-teens, his ambition to become a poet was unalterable.

By 1913 Esenin was permanently in Moscow, enrolled as an auditor, where he remained for one-and-a-half years, at the A. L. Shanyavsky Moscow City People's University, and working for a very short time in the butcher shop that employed his father and then as an apprentice proofreader in a printing house. The printing house was Russia's largest, printing a full one-fourth of all Russian books. The university was a remarkable educational institution whose doors were open to anyone "with a thirst for knowledge," a kind of free university in today's terms. (The main building, which opened in 1912, is now home of the Russian State University for the Humanities.) It was here that Esenin was exposed to world literature, taking inspiration particularly from Wilde and Whitman.

Esenin was writing poetry from a very early age and was already publishing, in the children's magazine "Mirok," before he turned twenty. His first collection of poetry appeared in 1916. It was not long before his work was noticed by his contemporaries, among them author, poet and playwright Anatoly Marienhof (1897-1962), who championed his work and became a lifelong friend and protector. They shared an apartment in the autumn of 1919 (that is to say, Esenin lived in the Marienhofs' apartment) and traveled the country together. Esenin dedicated a number of poems to Marienhof, among them one of his most famous, "I am the last poet of the village" (see page 88). Marienhof's own work subsequently came under severe attack by the Soviet politico-literary establishment, and these dedications were removed. (Marienhof's memoirs, published after Stalin's death under the title *My Century, My Youth, My Friends Both Male and Female*, contain many insightful recollections of Esenin.)

Esenin moved to St. Petersburg on 9 March 1915, and it was there that he started to adopt the appearances of a city boy, no doubt to hide his provincial roots. Later, however, he would sport many exotic guises on the streets of Moscow and the city that came to be called Leningrad—caps, hats, blue shirts, colorful ties, high-heeled yellow shoes, the whole eccentric and showy kit. He even donned a broad cape, conspicuously affecting the appearance of Pushkin.

He was desperate to be accepted in the highest ranks of Russian poets. He saw the two greatest poets of the day, Alexander Blok and Andrei Bely, as his rivals and equals, a most presumptuous notion for such a greenhorn from the Russian outback. His poems attracted a good deal of attention from other poets and writers, as well as being welcomed as fresh and inspiring by the public during the Silver Age (roughly the twenty-five years from the middle of the 1890s until the death of Alexander Blok in 1921).

Esenin was called to arms in March 1916. Needless to say, with his poet's temperament, he dreaded military service. But he had no choice. He was assigned work in a military sanitary train that was stationed at Tsarskoe Selo, the magnificent residence of the imperial family south of St. Petersburg.

The train, No. 143, was made up of twenty-one Pullman cars and was appointed in a luxurious manner. It was here that Esenin was to read his poetry to the empress on 22 July (see page 26). But before then the train had set out for Kiev and returned; and it was to make another trip during the war to Moscow, Kursk and points beyond.

Esenin served in the military for nearly a year, ending his service after the February revolution in St. Petersburg. It was thanks in part to his dear friend Nikolai Klyuev (1884-1937) that he had been able to avoid the front line. Klyuev and another one of Esenin's mentors, poet Sergei Gorodetsky (1884-1967), had sent a letter to a lieutenant whom they knew asking that Esenin be sent to Tsarskoe Selo.

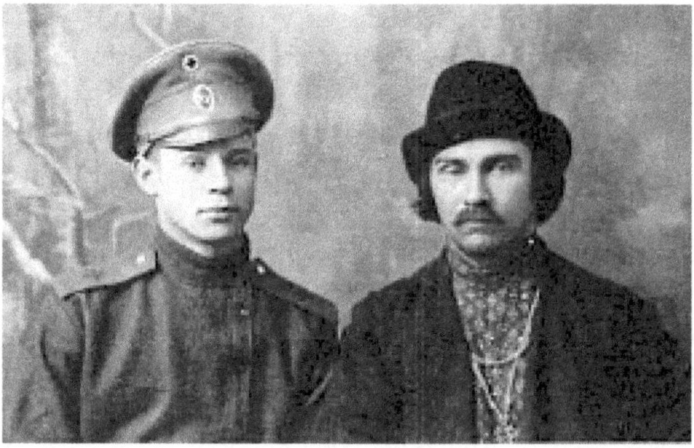

Of all the photos of Esenin that exist, the one of him in uniform, pensive and serene in his angled cap with its red cross over the hammer and sickle, is my favorite. Beside him is Klyuev, provincial dandy that he was, with a necklace hanging from the collar of his flowery rubashka.

During his service Esenin returned once to Konstantinovo, in June 1916 (see "I'm Here Again at Home With My Family," page 41).

Once out of the military and on his poetic feet again—by the end of the second decade of the century—Esenin was full of beans and quite ecstatic. He dressed from time to time in the country style, in rubashka, baggy trousers, kaftan and tasseled waistband, as if to say to all of Russia, "Take me as I am or not at all!" And most of Russia, in swift transition to becoming a modern industrialized nation state, was finding in Esenin's verse the means to bolster the conviction that the spiritual beauty of Russian nature was not going to be altogether lost.

Maxim Gorky remarked that Esenin looked like "a honey-colored postcard." Gorky, who was moved to tears when Esenin read "Song about a Dog" in Berlin, also remarked, looking back on his life and work, that "Esenin was not a man but an organ created by nature exclusively for poetry...." He might have added, "and for Russian posterity."

Even in his early poems Esenin described nature not only as a long mirror in space and time to view himself wholly, inside and out, but as an all-encompassing medium to bring together all human beings, animals, plants and the inorganic world of mountains, rivers and light into one poetic world—a world of his imagining. That world, I believe, retains its radiance and power to this day.

THE EVENING'S HERE

The evening's here. The dew
Glitters on the nettles.
I am standing by the road
Leaning against a willow.

Brilliant moonlight
Is striking our roof.
I can hear a nightingale singing
Somewhere far away.

I feel good and warm
As if beside a stove in winter.
The birches are erect
Like enormous candles.

Far beyond the river
And beyond the edge of the woods
The sleepy watchman clacks
His deathly rattle.

This poem was written in 1910, the year Esenin turned fifteen.

THE FLOOD FROM MELTING SNOW

The flood from melting snow
Licked the silt with its mist.
The moon shed
Yellow reins.

I'm traveling in a rowboat
Banging into the banks.
Russet haystacks stand like churches
Up at the drying racks.

Black wood grouse summon me
With their mournful cackling
To an all-night mass
In the quiet of the marshes.

Those mires conceal the poor
In their blue-black shadows.
I will say a secret prayer there
For your good fortune.

This poem is set in early spring, when the wood grouse mate. The male flaps his wings and makes a cackling sound that can be heard from more than two hundred meters away.

IT'S SNOWING CHERRY BLOSSOMS

It's snowing cherry blossoms.
The green is all blossom and dew.
Rooks pace the lanes of fields
Picking off wheat sprouts.

The silky grass droops.
The air reeks of pine resin.
Oh you, meadows and leafy woods ...
I am drunk on spring!

Secret tidings brighten my heart.
They shine right into my soul.
On my mind there's a wife-to-be.
It's solely of her that I sing.

Don't stop snowing down, you cherry blossoms!
And you, birds, sing out in the woods!
I'm going to ripple through these fields
Spreading flowers like foam.

BIRCH

White birch
By my window
Enveloped in snow
Yet silver too.

Tassels dangle
From its downy branches
A white fringe
On snowy hems.

The birch stands
In the silence of its slumber
And snowflakes burn
In a golden fire.

The dawn takes it time
In making its rounds
Sewing threads of fresh silver
Into all the branches.

This poem is much loved by Russian children, many of whom learn it at school and memorize it.

OH, I BELIEVE, I BELIEVE

Oh, I believe, I believe that happiness exists.
The light of the sun has not yet gone out.
The dawn prophesies blessed tidings
With its red prayer book.
Oh, I believe, I believe that happiness exists.

Ring out, ring out, golden Russia!
Blow up a storm, irrepressible winds!
Blessed are they who have celebrated with good cheer
Your shepherd sorrow.
Ring out, ring out, golden Russia.

I love the murmur of wild waters
And how a star shines in a wave.
The blessed suffering ...
The blessing nation.
I love the grumble of wild waters.

WAKE ME UP EARLY TOMORROW

Wake me up early tomorrow
My long-suffering mother!
I must go out to meet a dear friend
Past the burial mound by the road.

Today I saw wide-wheeled tracks
On the meadow in the depths of the wood.
The wind below a tent of clouds
Is buffeting its golden shaft bow.

The wind will dash away by tomorrow's sunrise
Lowering the moon, its cap, under a shrub.
And the mare will playfully flap
Her red tail over the plains.

Wake me up early tomorrow.
Turn on the light in our humble hut.
They say that I'll soon become
A Russian poet of great renown.

I will sing of you and my visitor friend
Of our stove, the rooster and the roof over our head ...
And the milk from your reddish cows
Will flow smoothly over my songs.

OLD RUSSIA

1

The village is sunk into ruts.
The woods shield its huts in their shadows.
All that can be seen from the tumps and the hollows
Are the skies showering the village with blue.

Menacing wolves howl in the gaunt fields
Throughout the long winter dusk.
Horses can be heard snorting over the eaves
In the burning frost of the homesteads.

Capricious ghost lights glimmer through the branches
Like owl eyes in a scarf of falling snow.
Tree stumps, akin to evil spirits of the forest
Stand beyond a netting of green.

A devil has frightened us
With ice holes and sorcerers wherever you look.
Galloons hang from the birch tree branches
In the misty dusk of the first autumn frost.

2

But how I love you, my meek and suffering homeland!
Yet I am at a loss to divine why.

Your short-lived spring merriment bursts in song
Across the meadows loud and clear.

I love to listen to the whine of the mosquitoes
When they swarm on the evening hay meadow.
And how the lads roar tunes on their concertinas
As the girls step up to dance around the bonfires.

Coal-black eyes burn under horseshoe brows
Like black currants set alight.
Oh you, old Russia, my beloved homeland!
Sweet is the sleep in the silk of your angelica.

3

The ravens have cawed out their omens
Of terrifying troubles sweeping the plains.
A maelstrom gyrates through the woods.
A shroud of spindrift skims over the lakes.

Thunder has clashed, shattering the cup of the sky.
Tattered clouds envelop the woods.
Celestial icon lamps on chains of fine gold
Swing fiercely to and fro.
Village constables have appeared at doorsteps
To call the men to arms.
The old tradesmen's wives babbled
As their wailing shredded the quiet air.

The peaceful young plowmen gathered together
And without a tear of sorrow or complaint
Stuffed their bags with sweet buns
Cramming them into their sturdy carts.

Everyone from the village and its outskirts showed up
To send them off to war.
That's your stout-hearted youths, old Russia
Coming to your aid in your day of misfortune.

4

The village pined like a young bride –
How were their loved ones so far away?
Why hadn't they sent any news?
Had they perished in the heat of battle?

The villagers imagined the smell of incense in the woods.
They imagined bones clacking in the wind.
And then came a pile of wondrous letters
With postmarks from parts faraway.

The young plowmen had not forgotten their loved ones.
They took pains to write to all their women
Who clutched their documents in their hands
Unable to unravel the knitted lines.

They squatted around the literate Lusha
For clues to what their loved ones were saying.
And listening to her read out the contents
They wept over the triumphs of their beloved he-men.

5

Ah, the fields and furrows that I love
How fine in your sorrow you are!
I love these ramshackle cottages too
Where gray-haired mothers wait by the door.

I kneel to kiss your birch-bark sandals.
Peace to you, scythe, rake and wooden plow!
I can read the fate of young husbands in battle
On the faces of their brides.

I've resigned myself to my weakness of spirit
Shrub by the river that I am.
But I want to share the hope of these women
As I light an evening star candle.

I've read the countless thoughts of these women.
Nothing terrifies them, not thunder, not dark.
They'll work the fields not brooding over prison or death
Singing songs of their secret desires.

They put their faith in those scrawled-out words
Copied down in painful labor.
And like the first rains that end a drought
Their tears of joy and fortune flowed.

And recalling parting with their loved ones
In the soft grasses under beads of dew
They imagined making hay on the meadow
A long way past the clouds of smoke.

Hey you, old Russia, my meek suffering motherland
All my love is saved for you.
Your thundering song on the meadow
Brings brief spring delight to the heart.

Esenin finished this long poem about his country at war at the beginning of 1915, prior to his move to St. Petersburg. His love of his country was boundless; it must have been, if it took in the whine of his region's horrendous mosquitoes.

This was one of the poems that Esenin recited personally to Empress Alexandra, wife of Tsar Nicholas II. She remarked that his poems were "beautiful but very sad."

"I replied to her," wrote Esenin in his short autobiography, "that all Russia is like that."

A COW

Decrepit, her teeth have fallen out.
The scroll of years reads on her horns.
The brutish herdsman beat her
Driving his cattle to pasture.

She's skittish when it comes to noise
Even a mouse scratching in the nook.
And she's plagued with terrible thoughts
About her little white-legged calf.

They didn't let her keep her first born.
Her rush of joy was for nought.
Now the wind whips the calf's hide
Impaled and hung beneath an aspen tree.

She soon will meet her son's fate
Once the buckwheat has been swathed.
They'll tie a noose around her neck
And lead her to the slaughter.

She'll be bitter, heartbroken and withered
As her horns bite into the dust
Dreaming the dream of a white grove of trees
And meadows of uncut grass.

THE WITCH

Her plaits are disheveled, she's white and horrible.
She runs frisky, she runs fast and bold.

The somber night is terrified into silence.
The moon is shrouded in shawls of cloud.

The wind sings out like howling old women
Racing into the thickest depths of the forest.

The spruce grove shakes its pike-like fists.
Owls stay hidden, shrieking from fear.

The witch waves her bony hands.
The stars blink through clouds over green woods.

Snakes dangle like earrings from her filthy locks.
She twirls with the blizzard, eerie and mad.

The witch dances to the knell of the pines.
Clouds float away, shuddering, black.

Apparently Esenin heard a description of a witch his mother once caught sight of. "We ran after her," his mother told him, "but she hid herself in a bank of morning fog."

THE BLIZZARD OF 26 APRIL 1912

What do you want, blizzard
Howling at my window?
You alarm a sick heart.
You sow grief and sorrow.

Don't linger here.
Let me lose myself in thought.
Can't you hear me? I'm weeping.
I'm repenting my sins before God.

Let me merge my soul and strength
With all the heat of prayer.
My spirit is spent and soon
My coffin will be closed.

Sing over me then
Only now move away ...
Or rather pray beside me
For my sinful soul.

IN MY LITTLE PEASANT'S HUT

The crumbly smell of wheat cake fills the room.
A tub of kvass sits by the doorstep.
Cockroaches slip through the cracks
In the molding round the stove.

Soot swirls above the damper.
Threads of ash lie on the grate.
The peelings of half-cooked eggs
Remain on the bench by the salt box.

Mother has trouble with the oven prong.
She bends down as low as she can.
The old cat creeps toward the pot
To get at the boiled milk.

The restless hens are clucking
Perched on wooden plow shafts.
And the cocks are singing in the yard
A harmonious liturgy.

Shaggy puppies by the vestibule window
Easily frightened by noise
Crawl out of their corners
Into a pile of horse collars.

Please forgive a translator's critical comment ... but can a poem be more painterly than this? This is a painting by a Dutch master in verse!

I AM A SHEPHERD

I am a shepherd and my chambers
Are bounded by rippling fields.
The slopes of the green hills resound
With the drumming of the great Russian snipe.

Clouds spin a lace of yellow foam
Above and around the woods.
I hear the pine trees whispering
Quietly dozing beneath the porch.

The green of the poplars glows
Beneath the dew in the shadowy dusk.
I am a shepherd and my grand old home
Is the fields with their soft green floors.

The cows carry on a conversation with me
In their language of nods and bows.
The scented green trees in the forest
Call out to the river with their branches.

I sleep on a heap of hacked out twigs
Oblivious to all human misery.
I pray to the scarlet dawn.
I receive communion by the brook.

GREEN HAIRSTYLE

Green hairstyle ...
Little chest of a young girl ...
Oh, skinny birch tree, what brings you
To gaze into the pond?

What is the wind whispering to you?
What's told in the ringing of the sand?
Or are your twigtails
Longing for a lunar comb?

Open, open up to me the secret
The timber of your thoughts.
I've fallen in love with the sounds
Of your late summer's sorrow.

And the birch tree answers me:
"Oh my inquisitive friend
A shepherd has been weeping
Under tonight's starry sky.

The moon has laid its shadows
And the green is all aglow.
He put his arms around my naked knees
And embraced me tightly.

And sighing deeply
He said under the chime of my branches:
'Farewell, my darling ... farewell
Until the cranes come back once more.'"

THE REEDS WERE RUSTLING BY THE INLET

The reeds were rustling by the inlet
As the lovely maiden princess wept by the river.

She threw her wreath of fortune into the water.
The wave unraveled its angel-hair braid.

"Don't get married, princess, in the springtime ..."
The wood demon spooked her with omens.

Mice have gnawed at the bark on the birches
Driven her out of the yard.

Horses fiercely toss their heads and fight.
Oh, how the house spirit despises black braids!

The pines in the grove pour forth their incense.
The ringing winds sing her requiem.

The young girl, downhearted, paces by the river
As spindrift from its waves weaves her shroud.

This poem alludes to the Thursday of the seventh week after Easter, when young girls adorned their heads with wreaths, the one here made from angel hair, or dodder. Then they would throw the wreaths into the river to see what happened to them, thus predicting their future. There was also a belief in Esenin's Russia that mice make an appearance on the threshing floor on this day, hence the reference to them in the poem.

A SHRUBLAND. THE STEPPE AND BEYOND

A shrubland. The steppe and beyond.
The light of the moon to the ends of the earth.
And again suddenly sleigh bells sob and wail
Overflowing into the night.

Our road may be unsightly
But it's ours to love forever.
Every Russian and his dog
Has traveled on this road.

And you, little sleighs! What sleighs you are!
And you, aspens, with your frozen jingles!
Oh, my old man was a peasant
And, by God, I'm a peasant's son.

I don't give a hoot in hell for fame
Or for being a poet.
But I haven't set eyes for ages
On this withered little land.

Anyone who's ever seen this land
With its fluid plains
Would gladly kneel before every birch
And kiss their little feet.

How can I hold back the tears
When the squeezebox sings in the frosty air
When the youth of the Russian village
Sing joyously in concert with it?

Oh you concertina, with your fatal poison!
The mad reputation of more than one man
Has been dashed to pieces
By the sound of your wailing call.

I'M HERE AGAIN AT HOME WITH MY FAMILY

I'm here again at home with my family
In my thoughtful and kind-hearted hometown.
Beyond the hill a verdant twilight
Waves its snow-white hand at me.

The gray-haired disheveled overcast day
Sails, ruffled, across the sky.
And the evening sorrow that descends upon me
Fills me with an insurmountable anxiety.

The shadows of sunset have fallen low
Over the onion domes of the church.
Oh my friends of holiday games and amusements
I will never see you again!

The years have gone into oblivion
And you have followed them somewhere
Leaving only the sound of water rushing
Beyond the sails of the mill.

And often in the gloom of evening
As the broken sedges rattle in the wind
I kneel and pray to the fuming earth
For those far away or gone forever.

I'M TIRED OF LIVING IN MY OLD HOMETOWN

I'm tired of living in my old hometown
Fed up with its vast buckwheat fields.
I'll just walk out of my little shack
And become a vagabond and thief.

I'll cut a path through the white curls of the day
And seek out some squalid place to live.
My dearest friend will sharpen his knife on his bootstrap
Readying it, no doubt, for me.

The yellow road across the fields
Coils in sunlight and spring.
But the one whose name is closest to my heart
Will chase me from her doorstep.

So I'll go back someday to the family home
Consoling myself with the happiness of others.
And on a green evening by my old window
I'll hang myself with the sleeve of my shirt.

The gray-haired willows along the wattle fence
Will bow their heads to me more gently than before.
And people will bury my unwashed body
To the barking of the dogs.

But the moon will just sail on and on
Dipping its oars into lake after lake ...
And old Russia will live on all the same
Dancing and weeping by the pales of its fence.

This poem seems, from its bleak perspective, to be a later piece, but it was first published in 1916.

MY BELOVED HOME COUNTRY!

My beloved home country! I harbor a dream in my heart
Of stooks of sunlight in womb-like waters.
How I'd love to lose myself
In your green cacophony!

Vestments of white clover and mignonette
Lie by the boundary pales of the fields.
Willows summoning with prayer beads
Stand together meekly, like nuns.

The marsh is burning a cloud of incense
Sending cinders up to the shadoof of Heaven.
And I've been harboring thoughts in my heart
A quiet secret for someone I know.

I encounter everything with open arms
And I delight in parading my soul.
I've come here onto this earth
To depart it as soon as I may.

Esenin loved to publicly recite this poem that is heavily infused with religious metaphors and similes. Among the numerous neologisms that he created in his body of work, one appears here, the word *stozvonnyi*, an adjective that breaks down to mean "having a hundred sounds." I rendered it here with "cacophony." Now, one might say that the sprouts and shoots of spring do not produce sounds. But Esenin hears them here and refers to such sounds in other poems as well. By "home country" he means the region in which he was born.

HEY YOU, OLD RUSSIA

Hey you, old Russia, my dearest family
Your huts are mounted icons.
You have no bounds, no visible end
Only dark-blue distance that drinks in the eye.

I gaze upon your fields
Like a pilgrim passing through.
Poplars wilt and jangle
On the splayed edges of the village.

In the churches your meek Savior
Smells of apple and honey.
The meadows are abuzz with joy
And the whirl of dance.

The laughter of young girls rings out
Reaching out to me like catkins
As I race down the beaten path
For the freedom of the green lynchets.

Were the Holy Army to cry out to me:
"Abandon old Russia and live in Paradise!"
I'd answer them, "I've no need for Paradise.
Just let me have my beloved homeland."

This poem describes Savior of the Apple Feast Day, celebrated and observed on 19 August in the Feast of the Transfiguration. This holiday custom, in which people eat apples and dishes made with apples, harks back to pagan times.

"Holy Army" refers to the legend of the army that followed Vladimir, the great prince of Novgorod and the ruler of Kievan Rus at the end of the tenth century, when Russia was first Christianized.

SILVERY ROAD

Silvery road
Where are you summoning me?
A single star is burning over you
A Holy Thursday candle.

Are you giving warmth to sorrow or joy?
Or are you steering the race to insanity?
Help me with your spring-like heart
To love your harsh snows.

Give me the dawn for a sleigh
And a willow switch for a bridle.
Who knows, I may just drive myself
To the very gates of heaven.

Another of Esenin's extraordinary usages occurs in this poem in the word *chistochetvergovaya*, an adjective that refers to Great Holy Thursday, or Clean Thursday (Maundy Thursday) in the Russian Orthodox Church. On the evening of this day parishioners hold candles during the service and then take them home to light their own icon lamps. In Esenin's time believers drew crosses on their doorways with the soot produced on the day.

PART TWO

His Times

"In the years of the revolution I was entirely on the side of October, but I took everything in my own way, with a peasant's bias."

Esenin was by no means unique in having an old-fashioned bias vis-à-vis the Russian revolution. The most famous poem of the early years of the revolution, Alexander Blok's "Twelve," published in March 1918, portrayed a march by twelve aggressive Bolsheviks likened to the twelve apostles of Christ, a message that is pronounced by the presence, at the end, of Jesus Himself leading the procession.

Like Esenin, experimental and popular novelist Boris Pilnyak (1894–1938) saw the forced mechanization of the countryside as a mixed blessing. Pilnyak wrote to a friend in 1924 that he felt a duty to be honest with himself and his country. (Esenin might just as easily have made this statement.) This sense of duty was to become an impossibility as Stalin tightened his grip on every aspect of life in the country in the 1930s; and Pilnyak, who had traveled to Japan and written a book and a series of articles, some of them in the Japanese press, praising that country's sleek modernization, was arrested on 28 October 1937. Chief among the charges was "spying for Japan."

The Supreme Court of the USSR sentenced him to death on 21 April 1938 after a "trial" that is said to have lasted fifteen minutes, and he was shot that very day in Moscow. (He was officially rehabilitated on 6 December 1956, soon after the leader of the Soviet Union and First Secretary of the Communist Party, Nikita Khrushchev, delivered his stunning watershed speech at the Twentieth Party Congress denouncing Stalin's regime of oppression and murder.)

Pilnyak, like Esenin, had made a trip to the United States and written a book about his experiences there, titled, with blatant irony, *Okay*. His impressions of the country are not at all okay. In a similar way to Esenin, he depicts Americans as "crassly materialistic." (Not surprisingly, *Okay* became one of several of Pilnyak's books translated into Japanese, appearing—with its negative slant on the U.S.—in 1941.)

As for Esenin, he too had few good things to say about the West in general; and though he was hardly a spokesman for his country's radical causes at the time, he was an ardent and loyal citizen in his own way. The trip abroad in 1922-23 only confirmed to him this loyalty, a loyalty, however, that he was equally wont to doubt.

He caused a great deal of trouble, especially in Berlin and Paris where he was often drunk and violently unruly. He was traveling with his wife, the American dancer Isadora Duncan, and overnighting in grand style. In Berlin, for instance, they lived in the luxurious Hotel Adlon on Unter den Linden. The list of guests who stayed there before the hotel was destroyed at the end of the Second World War includes many world-famous people. As for Esenin, he was uncomfortable wallowing in such luxury, and after his return remarked how put off he was by his mad Isadora's nearly two dozen suitcases and trunks. While in Berlin he walked out of the hotel one day and did not return. Isadora spent three days combing the city until she found him and dragged him back.

Needless to say, seeing as Esenin did not speak any language other than Russian and was prone to extreme antics and drunken binges, Berliners could hardly be blamed for coming to the wrong conclusions about his personality and loyalties. The press painted him up as a Chekist. (A Chekist was a person working for the Cheka, or Emergency Commission, the first of a series of state security organs that morphed into the KGB and, eventually, today's FSB.). Esenin was amused by this publicity and enjoyed presenting himself in top hat and tailored suit to confuse the people of the bourgeois West.

While abroad he deliberately provoked people. He attended a group meeting of émigré writers in Berlin, which was then the capital of exile for Russian intellectuals, angering them by calling for the playing of "The Internationale."

Esenin's circle of friends and admirers was enormous. In a letter written in Russian to Isadora on 29 August 1923 he tells her, "I was with Trotsky. He treats me amazingly. Thanks to his help, I'm now getting great ways to reach publishers. ... I wish you success and health and less vodka."

This was after they had returned to Moscow from their trip to Europe and the U.S. They were embroiled in one of their lengthy and legendary fights. Duncan left for the Caucasus around the middle of August. This separation proved permanent.

A few words about their journey overseas may shed light on how alienated Esenin was from Western values. The couple flew out of Leon Trotsky (!) Airport on 10 May 1922, bound for Königsberg. From Königsberg they took the train to Berlin.

After a stay in Berlin they traveled to Cologne, Strasburg and on to Belgium and Holland. They then based themselves in Paris, with a side trip to Italy.

Isadora was scheduled to perform in the U.S., but the pair were held up at Ellis Island while Esenin was interviewed. The official asked him if he believed in God, and the poet answered, "Yes." Then he asked him what "power" he recognized. Esenin replied, "The power of the people." This was a clever answer, as Lincoln as it was Lenin, and he was allowed entry into the United States.

The two went straight from Ellis Island to the Waldorf Astoria on

Fifth Avenue. (The building was taken down in 1929; now the Empire State Building stands on the spot.) After New York they went to Boston, Cleveland, Milwaukee and Detroit. He played the disgruntled tourist while she danced. He could barely cope with traipsing around the U.S. as "Isadora Duncan's young Bolshevik poet husband." If there was one instrument that Esenin was loath to play, whether in Russia or overseas, it was second fiddle.

During the NEP (New Economic Policy) instituted by Lenin to attract foreign capital to Soviet markets and boost the domestic economy, strict interpretations of ideology were not the iron-clad norm. This was an era where polemics played a major part in all aspects of life, both private and public. Socially the era was as much like the Swinging Sixties as the Roaring Twenties. A healthy freedom of expression, later to be regretted by many who availed themselves of its pleasures, was evident on the pages of books and the stages of theaters.

Esenin clearly availed himself of this freedom with relative impunity until ideologically motivated attacks on him became more virulent in the final months of his life. He published in journals and editions of various political leanings. But he considered himself above all ideologies, fond of playing the Red when in the West and the noncommittal fellow traveler at home. He saw himself solely as the spokesman for the old—read "real"—Russia. This self-image, rigorously nurtured and pursued by him, is what the Party sought to destroy in his final years and in the decades after his death. Nothing, not even someone's purist notions of what constituted "country," could ever rise above the Party. The state paid for Esenin's funeral and laid him to rest, they thought, once and for all. It wasn't until 1955, two years after Stalin's death, that his life and work began to receive official commemoration.

A comment by Esenin about one of his acquaintances, the author Ilya Vardin, in a letter to his sister Ekaterina on 17 September 1924, illustrates his convictions ...

"All that he does in literary politics, he does as a sincere communist. There's one trouble: He loves communism more than literature."

This is one of the clearest statements by Esenin that no ideology can take precedence over art.

The life of Ilya Vardin demonstrates the precarious status of those who attempted to reconcile art with ideology. His real name was Illarion Vissarionovich Mgeladze, and he was a prominent Georgian Soviet critic, political polemicist and Chekist known as the "hard Bolshevik." But his opinion that the party should "hold tightly to the reins" of government while allowing fellow-traveler socialists to have a platform was rejected by Lenin himself as "wrong ... and formalistic." This rejection did not augur well for Vardin's future. He was arrested in 1935, given a ten-year prison sentence and shot in 1941, though granted, in March 1959, that slight afterthought of Soviet empathy, "posthumous rehabilitation."

Esenin was often accused of anti-Semitism and was even arrested for displaying it. He did unashamedly use the Russian equivalent of the word "Yid." It is no secret that Russia has a long history, particularly in the countryside, of anti-Semitism. In the early years after the revolution attempts were made by the Party, with its many high-ranking Jewish officials and leaders, to banish this scourge. Of course, it was fashionable to be racist against all sorts of ethnicities and creeds at the time in the West as well as anywhere else. As for Esenin, his defensive pleading that "most of my lovers are Jewish"—which was true—sounded as if he was just substituting "lovers" for "best friends."

Esenin joined forces with the Imaginists, among them his close friends Anatoly Marienhof and Rurik Ivnev (1891-1981). The playwright Nikolai Erdman (1900-1970) was also a member of the group. (Erdman's classic satirical play *The Suicide*, about a man whose alleged suicide causes many people to claim its motivation as support for their cause, may very well have been inspired by Esenin's suicide.) The Imaginists were writers who saw themselves as creating a new avant-garde that gave free rein to guests in "The Hotel for Those Who Journey in Beauty" (the name of their journal). But Esenin was, by nature, not a person who could fit in within any constraints, however loose and sympathetically conceived they may have been. Even though he enjoyed the soirees at the Imaginists' café, Pegasus's Stall, I think he associated with his fellow Imaginists as much out of the loyalty of friendship, particularly with Marienhof, as dedication to the poetry of his peers in the group. He had little time for what he saw as the bourgeois and superficially Bohemian trappings that surrounded the group.

Another great friend and supporter of Esenin and his poetry was the poet Nikolai Klyuev. Eleven years Esenin's senior, and also hailing from the countryside, Klyuev took him under his wing. The men lived together in Klyuev's apartment in the autumn of 1915, and it is more than likely that they had an affair. Klyuev was openly gay at a time when sexual freedom was much more acceptable in Russia than it is today. Klyuev was not only a gifted poet but also a man who greeted the revolution in a similar manner to Esenin, as if it was a holy cause, with the emphasis more on "holy" than on "cause." Esenin responded passionately to this poet who wrote, "We are the grandsons of the earth...." When visiting friends, Klyuev would lay his head on Esenin's shoulder and stroke his hair. This tenderness did not deter Esenin from going out to seek female company, sending poor Klyuev into dour fits of jealousy.

Nikolai Klyuev was arrested in February 1934, freed and rearrested in June 1937. In October 1937 he was shot and buried in Tomsk.

The Imaginists continued to function haphazardly as a group throughout 1925 but they expired together with Esenin at the end of that year, though the association itself wasn't "liquidated," to use the word that appears in Russian sources on the Imaginists and many other groups, until the summer of 1927. Poet, author and translator Nadezhda Volpin (see page 95), with whom Esenin had a son (see page 96), continued to consider herself an Imaginist for years after the official death of the movement.

Esenin's trip abroad in 1922-23 with his wife at the time, Isadora Duncan, convinced him of his Russianness, which was then, willy nilly, connected at the feet, hip and shoulders to Soviet ideology. It was getting harder and harder not to march in step. Reading Esenin's letters to his friends back home during his long trip overseas gives the strong impression that he rejected the life and art of what he saw as philistinism. It seemed to him that all Europeans and Americans were petit bourgeois and narrow minded, gorging themselves on food and drink and dancing the foxtrot. Russia may be poor, but its people have a "soul."

He wasn't the first Russian artist to sulk in the refuge of that most acclaimed of spiritual apocrypha, the "Russian soul." It was something that he had fallen back into not only when overseas but also when walking the alien streets of Moscow and St. Petersburg. Perhaps it was the only thing, couched in a metaphor, you couldn't take away from him: the vessel in which resided his roots, his wooden *izba* (cottage, hut) and the sturdy old roof he had constructed in verse to house and preserve them.

He had written lines extolling Lenin. He had tried to create a march of the peasants, like Blok's faithful parade, toward the shining light of communism. He had written, in 1918, an epic narrative poem, "Inoniya," envisaging a utopian state. But it wasn't on. His heart and soul, as he more and more came to see them, were forever to reside in the refuge of that little cottage in old Russia, his true homeland.

But he increasingly came to feel, as he wrote in a poem, "a foreigner in my own land." By 1922 he would write, "I am ceasing to understand to what revolution I belonged." He flirted with the powerful, as did his friend, brilliant short story writer Isaac Babel. But such ties did not protect Babel, who was executed in 1940, and they probably would not have saved Esenin either had he lived long enough to be killed. He had read his poetry to Red Army commander Mikhael Frunze and Leningrad Party chief Sergei Kirov. Both men were murdered:

Frunze on the operating table (there for an operation he did not need) in 1925; and Kirov by a bullet in 1934.

Had he survived to see Stalin's merciless decimation of the peasantry he would not have strayed into any line of any parade. Had Russia taken another path, one of socialist progress based not on the sacrifice of all individual freedom for the "good" of the masses but on an inherent belief in the worth and welfare of every individual and the integrity of the environment, then Esenin would have, I believe, championed his country's causes. He had one foot decidedly and firmly planted on the new side of the river, as he kept the other on the old. Sergei Esenin may have been a reluctant warrior for Soviet-style progress, but he was no champion of the ancien régime.

Alas, he came to write ...

Who am I? What am I? Merely a dreamer
Who has lost the blue in his eyes to darkness....

He could have been the old plank bridge itself, to borrow a phrase from one of his most famous poems (see page 88), linking the old and the new Russias. But the gap between the sides was ever widening, causing him to lose his foothold on both. Not long after his death, the old Russia was all but destroyed and the new Russia was more terrifying than any imaginable reality.

At least Sergei Esenin, like his great and powerful rival Vladimir Mayakovsky, another suicide, decided his own fate before it could be decided for him by others with little trace of a heart and no soul at all.

CANTATA

Sleep, dear brothers.
Our native land mobilizes once more
Unshakable armies
Under the Kremlin walls.

New things are astir in the world.
The sky glows with red lightning.
Sleep, dear brothers
Sleep in the light of your incorruptible tombs.

The golden seal of the sun
Stands guard at the gates.
Sleep, dear brothers.
An army of people is on the move

Toward the universal dawn of nations.

There were elaborate celebrations in Moscow on 7 November 1918, the revolution's first anniversary, and Esenin was in attendance at the parade. Lenin had unveiled a statue of Marx and Engels beside the Bolshoi Theater before proceeding to the Kremlin where he delivered a speech honoring those who lost their lives for "peace and the brotherhood of the people," ie the revolution.

A cantata was sung at the unveiling of the plaque dedicated to those martyrs. The plaque featured a sculpted figure of a bare-breasted woman with the sun shining behind her. Esenin's adulatory cantata was part of the piece performed for the ceremonies by a choir made up of workers.

WORLD OF SECRETS

World of secrets, ancient world of mine
Like the wind you have settled down and stilled.
Now the stone hands of the highway
Are poised at the village's throat.

A ringing terror rushed in panic
Into the white-washing snow.
Hello there, my black destruction and death
I'm setting out to meet with you!

City, city, you christened us Carrion and Scum
In the grip of a brutal clash.
The field is choking with telegraph poles
Languishing in bull-eyed angst.

The devil's neck is sinewy and strong enough
To easily lay its iron logs across the marsh.
So what of it? It's not the first time for us
To be knocked loose and disappear.

This song sings of savage rights
However hard on the heart it may be.
When hunters hunt out their wolf
They surround him to close their vice.

The beast crouched down … and out of the dreary depths
Someone will pull a trigger.
The wolf suddenly leaps, as his fangs
Tear his two-legged foe to pieces.

Oh, good day to you, my favorite beast!
You don't yield to the knife just like that.
I, like you, have been chased into a corner
As I pass amongst iron-clad enemies.

I, like you, am always prepared.
As soon as I hear the triumphant horn
I will taste the blood of my enemy
In my final and fatal leap.

Let me fall in the loose whiteness.
Let me bury myself in the snow.
Yet a song of revenge for my death
Will be sung on a faraway shore.

This poem, written in 1921, describes the bloody civil war that broke out after the revolution. This war, still going on at the time of the writing of the poem—it didn't end until 1922—produced a death toll upwards of ten million people, most of them civilians who were either killed or died of illness or starvation.

STANZAS

I am well acquainted
With my own talent.
It's no big deal to write poems.
But what tormented
Stung and plagued me
More than anything
Was my love for my native land.

Anybody can put together
A few words that rhyme …
About a girl, the stars, the moon.
But a different sense
Devours my heart.
Different thoughts
Crush my skull.

I want to be a bard
And a citizen
The pride and exemplary model
To everyone
A real son
Not a stepson
In the great states of the USSR.

I ran away from Moscow for a long time …
I just don't have the knack
Of getting along with the police.

On every one of my scandalous binges
They threw me
Into the slammer.

I thank these uniformed citizens for their friendship.
But it's pretty hard
Sleeping on one of their benches
And reciting some poem
In a drunken voice
About the caged lot
Of a pathetic little canary.

Whatever you think, I'm no canary!
I am a poet!
And don't put me in the same camp as Bedny.
Though I may find myself stewed on occasion
My eyes are filled
With the light of marvelous worlds.

I see everything
And understand with perfect clarity
That we are living in a new era …
It's nothing to sneeze at …
That the name of Lenin
Rushes like the wind over the nation
Propeling our thoughts
Like windmill sails.

Spin, revolve, dear windmill wings!
You're in the wind today.
I am your nephew
And you all are my uncles.
C'mon, Sergei
Let's sit down quietly and read our Marx …
Take a whiff of the great wisdom
In dull lines.

Days run like streams
Merging into the fog-bound river.
Towns and cities flash by
Like letters on a page.
I was recently in Moscow
And here I am in Baku.
Chagin enlightens me
On the finer elements of drilling.

"Look," he says
"Don't you find these rigs
Gushing black fountains of oil
Superior to churches?
We've had our fill of your mystical fogs.
Sing, poet, in praise
Of what is more durable and real!"

Oil covered the water
With its Persian rug

As the evening was spilling a sack of stars
Throughout the sky.
But I am prepared to cross my heart
And swear that the refinery lights outshine
All the stars in Baku.

My head is full of thoughts of industrial might
And I hear the voice of human powers.
We've had our fill
Of all the heavenly lights.
It's easier to organize
Such things on Earth.

And so I say
While patting myself on the back
Of my neck:
"C'mon, Sergei
Let's sit down quietly and read our Marx.
The time has come
To divine
The great wisdom in dull lines."

This poem, published in October 1924, set in motion a storm of controversy, due to its irony and seemingly half-hearted enthusiasm for Soviet progress (see "May First" on page 77). Esenin dedicated this poem to his friend in Baku, Pyotr Chagin (1898-1967), who, by the way, was also a personal friend of the third-rate poet Demyan Bedny (see note on page 76).

THE ROGUE

The wet brooms of the rain sweep the meadows
Of droppings from the osier beds.
Spit out your armfuls of leaves, wind!
I, just like you, am an unruly rogue.

I love it when the dark-blue trees of the forest
Go down on their knees and soil their trunks
Just as lumbering oxen do
When their stomachs are groaning with leaves.

You are here before me, my red-brown herd!
Who could sing your praises better than me?
I see, yes, I see the twilight licking
Human footprints from the earth.

My old Russia, my old wooden Russia!
I am your sole poet and apostle.
I have nursed the melancholy of my feral poems
On your mignonette and mint.

Go, midnight, and fetch the moon's pitcher
To ladle up our birch tree's milk.
It seems the village cemetery is trying to strangle someone
With the arms of its crosses.

A black horror is wandering the hills.
A thief's spite streams through our garden.
But I'm the robber and rake
The rustler of the steppe by blood!

Who but me has witnessed an army
Of frothing bird cherry trees burning in the night?
I'd stand in that night with my flail in hand
Somewhere on the light-blue steppe.

Ah, the blond bush on my head has faded
And the prison of song has sucked me dry.
I've been sentenced to the hard labor of sensing
Keeping my poetic millstones grinding.

But do not fear, insane wind.
Calmly spit your leaves over the meadows.
I, like you, am a rogue in song …
And being called a poet
Will not erase me from the earth.

The Russian title of this poem is "Khuligan," a cognate of the English word "hooligan." While the Russian word is often rendered in English as hooligan, this has always seemed to me to be not quite right, a bit of a faux ami. The Russian word is much more widely used, even in a social and legal sense to describe rowdy or violent behavior. I've chosen "rogue" because it seems to fit Russian society's view of Esenin at the time, as well as the poet's own take on himself.

THE HOMECOMING

I went back to all the old places
To the village, the patch
Where I once lived as a little boy
Where the belfry, now missing its cross
Shoots into the air like a birch-wood fire tower.

How much had changed there
In the unsightly misery of those lives!
Revelation after revelation
Followed at my heels.

As for the home I was born in
I couldn't recognize it.
The big old maple was no longer swaying by the window
And mum was not in her chair on the porch
Tossing fine-grained kasha to the chickens.

She's of course put on years
Yeah … years and years.
I take in the surroundings with a heavy heart.
How unfamiliar it all looks to me now!
One thing, though, remains the same:
The tall gray boulder still stands
At the foot of the white hill.

And here's the cemetery
With its rotting crosses
Frozen with their arms outstretched
Like dead soldiers after hand-to-hand battle!
An old man with a stick is hobbling down a path
Brushing dust off the tall weeds as he goes.
"Hey, old man, would you be so kind
To tell me where I can find
The home of Tatyana Esenin?"

"Tatyana … hmmm …
It's that little cottage over there.
So what are you?
A relation?
Could you be the hopeless son?"

"Yeah, that's me, the son.
But what's it to you, old man?
Why are you staring at me
As if you were mourning me too?"

"Well good for you, good for you
For not recognizing your own grandpa!"
"Oh, Grandpa, can it really be you?"
And sad words flowed in warm tears
That fell onto the dust-covered flowers.

* * *

“I’d reckon you’re pushing thirty.
Well, I’m already ninety …
With one foot in the grave.
You should’ve come back long ago.”
He keeps knitting his brow.
“Yep, time … time!
You’re not a Communist, are you?”
“No!”
“Well, your sisters have joined the Komsomol.
Makes me sick to my stomach! Revolting!
They yanked the icons off the shelf last night
And the commissar’s removed the cross from the church.
There’s nowhere now where a man can pray to God.
So I steal myself into the woods.
I pray to the aspens
Hoping it’ll get through.

Come home with me.
You’ll see everything for yourself.”
So we set out, trampling on the roadside corncockle.
I throw a smile to the plowed land and the woods
While grandpa peers with melancholy at the bell tower.

* * *

"Hey, Mum, it's good to see you!"
And again I tug my handkerchief to my eyes.
Even a cow would find itself sobbing
At the sight of this poor little place.

Lenin on a calendar adorns the wall.
My sisters choose to live with this
My sisters, not me.
Yet I am ready to fall to my knees
When I gaze upon you, my beloved countryside.

The neighbors dropped in …
A woman with her baby.
Nobody recognizes me here anymore.
Only our old dog, as Byron wished for himself
Has met me at the gate with a woof.

Ah, my beloved land, my home!
What has become of you?
What is all this I see?
Sure, I know that I've changed too.
My sister smiles a happy smile
Though our poor mum and grandpa have no hope.

Of course, even Lenin is for me no icon.
I've seen the world …
I love my family …
But for some reason I find myself bowing
As I sit down on the old wooden bench.

"So, let's hear it, Sister!"

And so my sister opens her copy
Of *Das Kapital*, as if it were a Bible
Going on about Marx
About Engels
Whose works, whatever the times
I naturally haven't read.

And it makes me laugh
When such a clever little girl
Keeps grabbing me by the scruff of my neck….

* * *

Only our old dog, as Byron wished for himself
Has met me at the gate with a woof.

The Lord Byron reference is to his "Adieu, Adieu! My Native Shore" from *Childe Harold's Pilgrimage*. *Childe Harold* was wildly popular in Russia from the time it was published in the second decade of the nineteenth century.

Komsomol is the abbreviated name of the All-Union Leninist Youth Communist League.

GLORIOUS PUBLISHER!

Glorious publisher! I commit myself
To new feelings in this book.
Every instant takes me closer to a feeling for Russia
Old Russia spurred on by the commune.

Say that my pencil failed to whisper
Many things to the paper that it brushed
That my soul, half slumbering, sang hoarsely
Without comprehending our great festival.
But you too have the vision of a poet
And you will read my words between their lines.
You know that there's a new language
In the land where the Soviets rule.
And deciphering my bold experiment
You won't commit me to ridicule
Simply because my pencil failed to whisper all
To the paper that it brushed.

THAT HURRICANE HAS PASSED

That hurricane has passed. Not many made it through.
Few stepped up to the roll call of friendship.
Once again I've returned to my orphaned village
Where I haven't been for eight years.

Who can I call upon? Who will share with me
The melancholy joy that I have remained alive?
Even the mill, the one-winged timber bird
Stands with its eyes firmly shut.

Nobody here recognizes me
And those who can recall have long forgotten.
Where my family home once stood there now lies ash
And a coat of dust kicked up from the road.

Yet life rages in full swing.
Old and young faces
Bustle about me
Though there's no one I can tip my hat to
No eyes I can find refuge in.

And thoughts swamp my brain:
What is a homeland?
Am I simply dreaming?
Nearly everyone here sees me as a sullen pilgrim
From God knows how far away.

But this is me!
Me, a citizen of this village
A village to be known someday for one thing only:
That here a woman once gave birth
To Russia's notorious minstrel.

The mind's voice mutters to my heart …
"Pull yourself together! Why are you so offended?
It's only that the village huts are burning
With the new light of another generation.

You've already begun to become old hat.
Other young men are singing other songs.
Those songs, you see, will be more engaging.
Their mother's not the village, she's in all the lands on earth."

Oh, homeland! What a laughingstock I've become!
The hollows of my cheeks are flushed and parched.
The language of my fellow citizens sounds so strange.
I feel a foreigner in my own land.

Before my eyes
The villagers have gathered at the council building
In their Sunday best as if going to church.
Their discussions about "loif" are couched
In ignoble gnarled phrases.

Now evening's here. The setting sun has splashed
The gray fields with gilt spread thin.
The poplars have planted their bare feet along the ditches
Like heifers waiting round a gate.

A lame Red Army soldier with sleepy mien
And brow wrinkled with memories
Pompously recounts about Budyonny
And how the Reds trounced the Whites at Perekop.

"We licked the bourgeois good, we did.
We done did it down in the Crimea."
The maples curl the ears of their long branches.
Old women exclaim appreciatively into the mute darkening air.

The Komsomol peasants come down from the hillside
Singing to an accordion for all they're worth
The rhymed propaganda of Demyan Bedny
Filling the valley with their rapturous cries.

So that's my country!
That's all I needed!
Did I ever scream friendship with the people in my verse?
My poetry itself is no longer needed here.
And, as for me, I'm dispensable as well.

So what now?!
Forgive me, my native refuge.
If I've been of some service to you I'm satisfied.
I don't care if they sing my songs today or not.
I sang out when I felt my country in pain.

I will accept everything.
I accept everything as it is.
I won't stray from the beaten path.
I'll give my entire soul over to October and May
But I won't surrender my precious lyre.

I will not hand over my lyre to others
Not mother, not friend, not wife.
The lyre entrusted her sounds solely to me.
She sang her tender songs solely to me.

Blossom, young people! Keep honing your bodies!
Yours is a different life, your song a different tune.
As for me, I'll walk alone toward unknown bounds
Having subdued my rebellious spirit forever.

But even when the day comes
That the hostility of all the tribes
Becomes a thing of our planet's past

And all lies and sorrow vanish …
I will still extol
With my entire being as a poet
The one-sixth of the world that is
The old country: Russia!

The following was written in the popular journal "Oktyabr" (October) shortly after the poem appeared …

"Where is Esenin heading now? It's no use to guess: Life will tell. If he returns to his path as the bard of the old village or the pub reveler, he'll be done for as a poet. If, however, he goes farther ahead on his own new path, the revolution will receive him as a new and exceedingly talented poet. We wish him every success on this new road."

By 1924 it had become clear that Esenin had found himself caught in a vice of his own manufacture. One side of the vice is the old village and his old poetic persona; the other, the new dynamic Russia of forced industrialization. Though he will express misgivings about his commitment to the old Russia, he knows all too well that he is unable to give up his drunken revelry in it.

He states in this poem that he hasn't been back home for eight years, but this is not true. He made a trip there four years earlier, in April and May 1920; and perhaps also visited a year or two after that.

Semyon Budyonny, eventually to become Marshal of the Soviet Union, fought the Whites during the Civil War at Perekop, gateway to the Crimea.

Demyan Bedny, who makes an appearance on page 63 as well, was a communist poet who wrote works of harmless insipid satire.

MAY FIRST

There's music, poetry and dances
And there's lying and flattery.
Let them curse and berate me for my "Stanzas."
The truth lies in them.

I've seen the May Day celebrations
And I am struck.
I was ready to die just to stroke
All those lovely girls and wives.

Wherever you go, whatever stories
You whine out
Is there anything like the sun over the lake
At Balaxani?

The anthem strikes fire in the heart.
The body trembles and shakes.
Forty thousand people marched and sang
And drank their fill to boot.

Poems! Poems! Don't overdo the "LEFt" business!
Keep it as simple as simple can be!
We toasted the health of the oil industry
And the company we are keeping.

And so, raising my first big glass
On this May Day Festival
I knocked it straight back
Toasting the Council of People's Commissars.

Keeping a low profile and still on my trolley
I drained the second big glass
Proudly toasting the workers
As someone droned on about something or other.

And I polished off my third big glass
Like a Central-Asian khan
Toasting an end once and for all
To the back-breaking lot of the peasantry.

Drink, drink, my heart! Just beware
You don't explode inside me.
So that's why I downed my fourth big glass
Solely for the benefit of myself.

Esenin found himself in Baku on 1 May 1925. He met, picnicked and drank with workers, many of whom knew his work well. His commitment to the cause of the dictatorship of the proletariat seems to become diluted by the fourth toast.

"Stanzas" refers to the poem beginning on page 60.

Balaxani is a municipality near Baku where, in 1837, the Russian mining engineer Nikolai Voskoboinikov built an oil refinery.

"LEFt" is Esenin's play on words on LEF, the Left Front of the Arts, the official organization, whose members considered it the only true representative of revolutionary art. It was founded at the end of 1922 and disbanded in 1929.

INDESCRIBABLE, DARK-BLUE AND GENTLE

Indescribable, dark-blue and gentle …
The calm of my home after thunder and storm.
My spirit is a boundless field
Breathing honey and roses.

I am calmed. The years have done their handiwork.
Yet I don't curse what's transpired.
It's as if a rabid troika of horses
Has swept over the whole country.

They have kicked up dust everywhere, leaving hoofmarks
In the earth, then died away to a devil's shrill whistling.
And now I can even hear a leaf fall
In this forest retreat.

Is that bells jingling? An echo from far away?
My heart drinks it in with perfect calm.
Pause here, my heart, for we have passed over
The turbulent path accorded us.

We'll deal with all that we've witnessed
With what the country's gone through
And we'll forgive those who have abused us
Through their fault or through our own.

I accept both what was and what wasn't.
But my sole regret in my thirtieth year
Is that I lost myself in the fumes of liquor
And asked too little of myself when young.

Until the young oak forms acorns
It bends like the grass in the field.
You too, my daredevil youth …
My golden tearaway youth.

By the time he wrote this poem—spring 1925—Esenin was having moments of equanimity when it came to what he and his country had been through. To my mind there may be no more telling comment about what transpired in Russia in the early years of the revolution than these in this poem: *It's as if a rabid troika of horses/ Has swept over the whole country.* Fortunately Esenin was not to see what followed in the decades after his death.

THE FEATHER GRASS IS ASLEEP ON THE PLAINS

The feather grass is asleep on the plains.
The wormwood smells fresh, like lead.
No other homeland can pour
Such warmth into my heart.

As compatriots we share, you know, a common fate.
And you can ask anyone
Whether rejoicing, rampaging or tormented
If they live a good life in our old Russia.

The rays of the moon are elongated and mysterious.
The willows weep and the poplars whisper.
And no one in this land will cease to love
The fields of home and the cry of the crane.

And now when my life has been touched by destiny
In the glare of a brave new light
I am nevertheless still the poet
Of the golden log hut of home.

In the nights when I snuggle up to my pillow
I see alien young people, a formidable foe
Spewing forth new-fangled gismos
Over my meadows and glades.

I can still continue to sing out with all my heart
Despite these encroachments of "novelty":
Just let me die still loving everything
Peacefully in my beloved homeland.

THIS FLUID MOONLIGHT DISQUIETS ME

This fluid moonlight disquiets me.
These endless plains depress me.
I wasn't alone in cursing
All that I saw in my fast youth.

The willows are withering by the roadsides
Where the song of cartwheels is heard.
I fervently wish now never
To hear that song again.

I've become indifferent to peasant hovels
And don't warm to the fires in their hearths.
Even a blizzard of springtime apple blossom
In a misery of fields leaves me cold.

My heart and soul are drawn elsewhere
In the consumptive light of the moon.
I now see the might of my native land
Built of stone and forged in steel.

Provincial Russia! You've had your fill
Of tugging your old wooden plow through the fields!
Even the birch trees and the poplars
Are pained to witness your poverty.

I have no idea what will become of me.
And perhaps I'm not fit for the new life.
And yet, in the end, I do wish to see
Poor wretched Russia made of steel.

I harken now to the automobile's bark
In the jostle of blizzards, the throes of storms.
And nothing can now make me listen
To the song of cartwheels on the road.

He wrote this poem in May 1925 and sent it to the influential literary journal "Novy Mir" (New World) in October. It was published in 1926, the year following his death.

THIS STREET IS SO FAMILIAR TO ME

This street is so familiar to me
As is this humble home.
Telephone wires hurtle over my window
Like a bundle of sky-blue straw.

There were years of oppressive disasters
Years of mad and violent forces.
I recall my childhood in the village
I recall it in watercolor blue.

I sought neither fame nor tranquility.
I'm familiar with the vanity of fame.
And now when I close my eyes
All I see is my childhood home.

I see the garden speckled light blue
With August curled up quietly against the wattle.
In their green paws the lindens embrace
A twittering hubbub of birds.

I so loved that wooden home
With awesome wrinkles glimmering in its logs
With our stove wailing wildly and eerily
Long into the rainy night.

Its voice was loud and its sobbing full throated
As if mourning someone living or dead.
What could this brick-red camel be seeing
In this rain-sodden howling?

It's clear that it saw lands far away
Some other dream of flourishing days
The golden sands of Afghanistan
And a glassy Bukhara haze.

Ah, I too know those distant lands.
I've been to not a few.
Yet now I'd like to turn on back
To the land of my childhood.

But that tender daydream has gone out
Burnt to ash in sky-blue smoke.
Peace to you, fields of straw.
Peace to you, my wooden home!

SNOW FLURRIES ARE SWIRLING IN A DANCE

Snow flurries are swirling in a dance
As a troika I don't recognize races over the fields.

Alien young people are racing this troika.
Where can I find happiness? Where lies my own joy?

Everything has driven off in a wild storm
On just this sort of frenzied troika.

I AM THE LAST POET OF THE VILLAGE

I am the last poet of the village.
The old plank bridge is humble in my songs.
Birch trees cense the air with their leaves
For my farewell mass.

My waxy flesh is a candle
Burning down in a golden flame.
And soon the moon, a wooden clock
Will gruffly strike my midnight hour.

It won't be long before the iron guest
Carves a path through the light-blue field.
Its blackened fists will scoop up
The oats spilt by the dawn.

These poems won't come alive
In alien palms dead to the world.
Only the horses pulling the reaper
Will grieve the loss of their old master.

The wind will suck away their neighing
As they celebrate the funeral with dance.
It's not long now till the wooden clock
Gruffly strikes my own midnight hour.

This poem, written on a visit home to Konstantinovo in 1920, is perhaps Esenin's most famous, if only for the fact that he is to this day referred to as "the last poet of the village."

The "iron guest" is industrialization.

PART THREE

His Loves

Esenin's love life was complicated to say the least, even in an era of revolutionary change and freewheeling indulgence in the intimate affairs of men and women.

The women who played a major romantic role in his life were:

Anna Izryadnova (1891-1946)
Zinaida Raikh (1894-1939)
Galina Benislavskaya (1897-1926)
Isadora Duncan (1877-1927)
Nadezhda Volpin (1900-1998)
Sofia Tolstaya (1900-1957)

He was married to Izryadnova, Raikh, Duncan and Tolstaya and lived for a time with Benislavskaya and Volpin. There were other romances in his life, particularly with the beautiful actress Avgusta Miklashevskaya (1891-1977), to whom he dedicated seven love poems, including "Come and Sit Beside Me, Darling" (see page 100) and "Don't Torment Me With That Coolness Of Yours" (page 123).

Avgusta, who worked under the eminent theater director

Alexander Tairov (1885-1950), artistic director for many years of the Kamerny Theater, had been introduced to Esenin by Marienhof's wife, Anna. Avgusta later wrote of their first meeting, toward the end of the summer of 1923, that he was pale and steeped in thought as he walked swiftly down Tverskaya Street. She noticed his gorgeous "golden" hair and that he barely paid any attention to her.

The two subsequently met at the Marienhofs' apartment where he often spent the night. He was still technically married to Isadora Duncan, but the marriage was clearly on the rocks. Avgusta could see how ecstatic he was to be back home in Russia after his long trip overseas and how inextricably tied he was to everything Russian. To Esenin, even the moon looked different over Russia.

However close their relationship was in spirit, Esenin's romantic passes went largely unrequited … hence, the "coolness" in the poem. In 1976 Avgusta, age eighty-five, claimed that they had never even kissed. As with most things exalted by him, the exaltation came from his imagination.

But back to the beginning.

Anna Izryadnova, a Moscovite, was working as a proofreader when the young Esenin, fresh from the fields, landed a job at the printing house. He was eighteen; she, twenty-three. Though he had just come up from the country, he strove to fit in with his brown suit, high starched collar and tie. Anna noted how arrogant he was and that his excessive display of amour-propre turned people off.

The two married in a civil ceremony in the autumn of 1913. Anna gave birth to their son Yuri in December 1914. (Yuri was arrested in April 1937 on charges of being "an active member in a counterrevolutionary fascist-terrorist group," taken to the Lubyanka Prison in Moscow, tortured until he wrote out a confession, shot, and posthumously rehabilitated in 1956.) Needless to say, Esenin was much too young and self-obsessed, already a self-styled "rogue" poet, to be a decent husband and faithful father. He walked out on them.

Zinaida Raikh was, by all accounts, the greatest love of his life. "A

Letter to a Woman" (see page 125), addressed to her, speaks volumes of an undying love. Isadora Duncan may have been the mother he had longed for ... but how deep is an ocean of two repelling tides, of waters so different that they can never truly come together and mix? It was Raikh who captured his heart. He would never love anyone as he loved Zinaida Raikh.

She is described by contemporaries as a woman radiating great charm with a come-hither look in her eyes; though Anatoly Marienhof, who profoundly disliked her and made no secret of the fact that he considered her talentless as an actress, said that her face was round, "like a plate." Raikh was very different in temperament from Esenin in that she craved luxury and obsessively fancied the good things in life—expensive furs and perfume, exorbitant hotel rooms—while all Esenin craved was a seat at a bar and the sympathetic ear of a stranger.

Their relationship was fraught with rows, as all of Esenin's relationships were with his women. When arguing, Esenin invariably turned nasty, with, according to Raikh, "the face of someone else, not his own," coming out with the crudest insults. This love-hate relationship may have been the only kind that Esenin was able to nurture; but the fact remains that he had settled down with no other woman, had what he would call a family and a home with no other woman than Raikh.

His outbursts with her were, at least in part, the result of a jealous rage. He claimed that she was receiving presents from lovers. He admitted that he beat both Raikh and Duncan, "because for me love is a terrible torment, sheer agony."

Zinaida Raikh was a striking woman whose face, despite its prominent jaw and chin, looked nothing like a plate. She and Esenin married in July 1917 and remained husband and wife for more than four years, divorcing in October 1921. (In 1920, however, Esenin was already living with Galina Benislavskaya.) Their daughter Tatyana (Esenin's mother's name) was born in May 1918; their son Konstantin (probably named after Esenin's village), February 1920. Tatyana, who became an author and a director of the Sergei Esenin Museum, passed away in 1992; Konstantin, who devoted his life to football, in 1986.

As for Raikh herself, she was murdered by multiple stab wounds to the face and body in her apartment in 1939. This was clearly carried out by hired agents. Her husband at the time, illustrious theater director Vsevolod Meyerhold, had been arrested less than a month before. His torture was particularly assiduous, forcing him into a confession as a spy for Japan and Great Britain. He was executed early the next year, and rehabilitated in 1955. Incidentally, Raikh was convinced that Esenin too had been murdered by the state.

Though Esenin had made a brave attempt at being a husband and father, he still flitted about in search of the limelight, racing around town in search of companionship, often followed by a bevy of ardent groupies.

Esenin's marriage to the famous American dancer Isadora Duncan has become a legend written about and commented on by a great many people. Some in Esenin's closest circle of friends, such as the Imaginist poet Rurik Ivnev, even blamed her for his suicide, which is quite a stretch.

Esenin and Duncan could not speak each other's language, which is probably why their marriage lasted as long as it did, not much more than a year. Here is an undated letter he wrote to her in early 1923 …

Isadora browning darling sergei lubich moja darling scurry scurry.

While it's hard to comment on the content of this letter, save to say that "browning" probably refers to a gun, it is equally hard to believe Esenin when he wrote, "It's better to see people and to speak with them with your lips, eyes and entire being than to produce those limited letters of the alphabet." He was, after all, a born wordsmith. It seems a rather paltry comment for a man who dedicated his entire being to those "letters of the alphabet."

"Isadora has a fiendish power over me," he confessed to a friend. "When I walk out, I think that I'll never go back again, but the next day or the day after that I'm returning to her. It often occurs to me that I hate her. She's so … alien! You understand, completely alien. I look at her and I find it almost ridiculous that she wants to be my wife. This woman? What's she to me? What am I to her? My poems … my name … I mean, I'm Esenin … I love Russia, cows, peasants, the village. And she loves Greek vases … ha … ha … ha. My milk turns sour in Greek vases. She has such empty eyes … such a strange face … gestures, voice, words … it's all strange and alien. And yet I return to her. She's very clever! And she loves me. Her eyes and her funny Russian move me. Sometimes I feel so good with her! Genuinely good! When we're alone … when we maintain silence … or when I read her my poems. … She loves me very much. Don't think it's because of money or because of fame! I spit on that! My fame is bigger than hers. I am Esenin!"

Isadora Duncan was born in San Francisco in 1877, some eighteen years before Esenin, and died in 1927 in Nice, France. Her death —she was strangled by a long scarf that became entangled in the spokes of the sports car she was a passenger in—was portrayed in Karel Reisz's 1968 film *Isadora*, in which she was played by Vanessa Redgrave. Esenin was played by the Croatian actor Zvonimir Crnko.

Esenin had transferred his affections to Isadora from Galina (Galya) Benislavskaya. Galina was hopelessly in love with him whatever he did; and she suffered, even as she watched him flit from one flower to the next right up to his death. Esenin once told his sister Ekaterina that he had said to Benislavskaya, "Galya, you are so good. You are my closest, best friend. But I don't love you as a woman. You should have been born a man."

How awful is that! And this is supposed to be a man who understands women?

Galina Benislavskaya shot and killed herself beside Esenin's grave on 3 December 1926, about three weeks short of the first anniversary of his death. She was twenty-nine.

Nadezhda Volpin was a brilliant young linguist, music teacher, translator and poet. During her long life, that lasted nearly a century, she knew many renowned poets beside Esenin, such as Mayakovsky, Mandelstam and Pasternak. She had studied poetry under one of the greatest poets of the era, Andrei Bely.

She met Esenin in late 1920 when she was drawn to the Imaginist group of poets, and the two had an on-again-off-again relationship for about three years. Nadezhda gave birth to their son, Alexander, in May 1924. By then Esenin had left her. When she told him that she was pregnant, he confessed to her that he already had three children. She had known about the two with Zinaida Raikh, but had never been told about the existence of his son Yuri.

Their son Alexander Esenin-Volpin died in March 2016 at the age of ninety-one. He had an amazing career as a mathematician and was an indestructible campaigner for human rights. Despite having undergone the torture of forced hospitalization in Soviet psychiatric clinics, he became one of Russia's (and America's, seeing as he became a citizen of that country) most highly esteemed champions of freedom and human rights.

Though Nadezhda and Esenin fought like the devil, he was less inhibited by his many complexes when in her presence than in the presence of other women. Nonetheless, he left her for the woman who became his fourth and last wife, the granddaughter of Lev Tolstoy, Sofia Tolstaya.

Sofia first set eyes on him in late 1921 when he was reading his poetry at Pegasus's Stall, but didn't actually meet him until 1925. He was living with his sister Katya (Ekaterina) at Galya Benislavskaya's apartment, where they often invited writers and literary colleagues. Sofia arrived with Boris Pilnyak, with whom she was having a relationship. When she was ready to leave in the middle of the night, Esenin offered to walk her home, and they roamed about the city for a long time. By the time they reached her home, she felt, as she wrote years later, that she was "destined" to be with him.

"Destiny" is the right word, for soon after that Esenin proposed marriage and she readily accepted. She was well aware of his mental problems, but convinced, in the beginning at least, that she could wean him off liquor and make him well.

They were married on 18 October 1925, which turned out to be two months and ten days before Esenin killed himself. Even though the marriage was shortlived, it was characterized by the same sort of bickering and fights he had had with his other wives.

Sofia was instrumental in having Esenin sent to the psychiatric clinic, as is discussed on page 131.

Benislavskaya had told him a year earlier that he had a devil inside him that he had to "drive out," assuring him that he could do it if he set his mind and heart to it. But could he have? He was fortunate in being blessed with so many friends and lovers propping up his confidence and giving him the hope to survive. Sadly, it wasn't sufficient to cure his illness or make him feel at home in the new Russia.

Esenin's most pure love was perhaps reserved for his sisters. On 10 August 1922, as he was about to leave Venice for Rome and then go by train back to Paris, he wrote to his sister Ekaterina that she should study hard and read books, warning her that in the school of life, "people are not always good."

I have divided, as best as I could, the objects of Esenin's affection into this order: women, men, his mother and family, and finally, animals, for whom he felt great affection and devotion. But there is also his profound love of, before all, the works of Nikolai Gogol and, not far behind, the poetry of Alexander Pushkin.

Both Gogol and Esenin were from the country and brought up past the far edges of cosmopolitanism, yet both aspired to life in the big city, especially St. Petersburg. The tone of their language is not mainstream Russian but rather provincial and somewhat foreign sounding when judged from the center. He called Gogol "my only teacher," though clearly Pushkin's love poems, as well as his sharp-tongued satirical ones, had a deep effect on him. His love of these two Russian writers pervades his verses.

I WON'T GO WANDERING

I won't go wandering, crushing saltbush under foot
Or search for your trace in those bushes.
With your sheaf of oat-colored hair
You are never out of my dreams.

With the scarlet juice of berries on your skin
You were soft and beautiful and tender.
You were radiant, you shone like the snow
Like the rose of the sky at sunset.

The grains of your eyes have crumbled.
Your delicate name has faded away like a sound.
But the smell of honey from your innocent hands
Has remained in the folds of a wrinkled shawl.

At the quiet time, when dusk is settling on the roof
I sit like a kitten washing its mouth with its paw
And I listen to the singing waters
Speaking serenely with the wind about you.

Let the dark-blue wind whisper to me
That you were a song and a dream.
But who thought up your supple figure and shoulders?
Who placed lips on that radiant secret?

I won't go wandering, crushing saltbush under foot
Or search for your trace in those bushes.
With your sheaf of oat-colored hair
You are never out of my dreams.

It is thought that the woman in this poem is a girl he knew in his home village, a girl who had passed away.

COME AND SIT BESIDE ME, DARLING

Come and sit beside me, darling
And let's look into each other's eyes.
I'm dying to listen to that sensual snowstorm
Swirling beneath your timid glances.

This autumn gold
And these strands of pale hair …
It all appears as a kind of salvation
For a restless and troubled rake.

I turned my back a long time ago
On my village, where the woods and meadows flower.
I wanted to live down and out
In the acrid fame of the city.

I wanted my heart to hark back less
To my summers and my gardens
To the time I trained myself to be a poet
Listening to the chorus of the frogs.

And now again the autumn's here
With its maples and lindens thrusting their branches
Like paws against our cottage windows
As if trying to reach those they recall.

But they're gone long ago now from the world.
The moon with its beams eyes the crosses
In the simple village graveyard
Tempting us to be guests there too

Inviting us who have gone through a hell of troubles
To take our place under its shelter of light.
All the undulating roads in the world
Pour bliss only onto the living.

Darling, sit down here beside me
And let's look into each other's eyes.
I'm dying to listen to that sensual snowstorm
Swirling beneath your timid glances.

A LIGHT-BLUE FIRE IS TOSSING AND TURNING

A light-blue fire is tossing and turning
And my faraway home is forgotten.
It's my first time to stop causing trouble.
It's my first time to sing about love.

I was like a garden gone to seed
Unable to resist my women and my poison.
Now I've ceased my boozing and dancing
And ceased tossing my life to the winds.

My sole desire is to gaze upon you
And peer into the hazel-gold depths of your eyes
So that you might come to rue the past
And stay with me forever.

Your graceful walk … your supple figure …
If you could only know in your heart of hearts
How a rake like me can love
How obedient and submissive he can be.

I'd never set foot in another pub
And pack in writing verse
Just to delicately touch your hand
And stroke your autumn-colored hair.

I'd follow you to the ends of the earth
Back home or wherever you wished.
It's my first time to stop causing trouble.
It's my first time to sing about love.

I'M PICKING REDDENING POPPIES IN THEIR BEDS

I'm picking reddening poppies in their beds
In my white kaftan and scarlet sash.
I can hear the bellowing village chorus in the distance.
I know that she is there … that she is singing in it.

I recall how she shrieked when stealing into my cabin:
"You're handsome, for sure, but I don't fancy you.
The rings of your curls have been burnt by the wind
But another man takes care of my sharp-tooth comb."

I know what's put her off about me.
I never danced as much or drank as hard as the others.
I stood meekly and wanly with my back to the wall
While all the men sang songs and got plastered.

It's the shameless one who's got the luck.
It's his beard that's brushed her neck.
And she burst into a laugh right in my face
When she joined him in the dance's fiery ring.

I'm picking reddening poppies in their beds
In my white kaftan and scarlet sash.
Her poppy heart is blossoming in love.
It's only that her song is for another.

YOU WEPT IN THE QUIET OF EVENING

You wept in the quiet of evening
Shedding bitter tears into the earth.
And I felt deeply sad and troubled
That we couldn't see eye to eye.
You have now sped away to distant parts
And all my dreams have withered, colorless.
Again I'm left alone to suffer
Without so much as a greeting or caress.
But when the days turn into night
I frequent all the places of our trysts.
I see your image in my dreams, my love
And hear your melancholy weeping in the hush.

THE LEAVES FALL AND FALL

The leaves fall and fall.
The wind moans
A slow prolonged and hollow moan.
Who will bring joy to my heart?
Who, my friend, will console it?

I stare and stare up to the moon
With weighed-down eyelids.
The raucous call of the roosters
Rocks the autumn-wrapped calm.

This dark blue before the dawn …
This blessed delight of streaming stars …
If only I could think up some sort of wish now …
I've no idea of what to wish for.

What to wish for in the grip of everyday burdens
While cursing my lot and my home?
What I'd fancy right now is catching sight
Of a good-looking girl just outside my window.

I'd wish for her to console me deep down
With her cornflower eyes
And her fresh words, her feelings …
Only me
No one else!

I'd wish that fate would smile down on me
In this white lunar luminescence
And that I wouldn't melt and swoon over my songs
And that faced with the happy youth of others
I would never regret my own.

SING FOR ALL YOU'RE WORTH

Sing for all you're worth and let your fingers dance
In a semi-circle on your damn guitar.
I would gladly suffocate in this hot stupor.
You are my last and sole friend in life.

Don't gaze at her slender wrists
Or the silk flowing over her shoulders.
I sought my happiness in that woman
But inadvertently found my own ruination.

I did not know that love is an infection.
I didn't know that love is a plague.
She came to me with one narrowed eye
And drove this scoundrel out of his mind.

Sing for all you're worth and bring on once again
Our wild and passionate dawn hours.
Who cares if she kisses another
That beautiful young piece of trash!

Oh, but stop. I'm not swearing at her.
Just stop. I'm not cursing her at all.
Just let me sing to you about myself
In harmony with these deep chords of the guitar.

The rose-colored cupola of my days streams by.
There's a bagful of gold dreams in my heart.
I've fingered the skin of many girls
And pressed women into many a corner.

Oh yes! It's one of this world's bitter truths
And I first watched it when a little boy:
The male dogs line up to lick
The juice that comes out of the bitches.

So why should I be jealous of her?
Why get all hot under the collar?
Our life is all just sheets and a bed.
Our life is but kisses and it's down the plughole.

Sing for all you're worth! A troubled fate resides
In the fateful sweep of these hands.
Just know this: The others can all go fuck themselves …
And that I, my friend, will live forever.

MY LOVE NOW IS NOT WHAT IT USED TO BE

My love now is not what it used to be.
Oh, I know how you grieve and grieve
Because bristles of the moon's broom have not scattered
The puddles of light that are poems.

You mourned, yet you found joy in a star
That fell onto your eyebrows.
And though you sang your heart out to your hut
You didn't make a home in that heart.

And that man whom you waited for at night
Passed right on by your shelter as before.
For whom did you gild your keys, my friend
With the words of your song?

You'll no longer be extolling the sun.
And you won't be catching sight of heaven in your little window.
The mill may flap its wings.
But it can never fly off this earth.

Esenin and the man for whom he wrote this poem, Nikolai Klyuev, had many affinities. Their poems resonated with words and images of the countryside, words such as *izba* (hut). In fact, both sang of "the little old huts of Russia" in a similarly plaintive and nostalgic way. When this poem was written—1918—they were, what might be called, "comrades in farms." As I have written above, it is fairly clear that they were comrades in each other's arms as well.

By 1920 the two men were falling out with each other, though Esenin's suicide in 1925 hit Klyuev very hard. Some of Klyuev's poetry, by the way, is superb. The two poets were the soul brothers of post-revolutionary Russia. Esenin seems to have attempted to reconstruct the friendship, but it never returned to the warmth of an earlier time. Esenin had found in Klyuev someone who instinctively understood him, and this alone attracted him to Klyuev's kindred spirit when he despaired in his black moods.

SHAGANEH, MY SWEET SHAGANEH

Shaganeh, my sweet Shaganeh
Could it be because I come from the north
That I'm eager to tell you of a field
Where moonlight ripples over rye?
Shaganeh, my sweet Shaganeh!

Could it be because I come from the north
That the moon there appears a hundred times more gigantic?
However beautiful Shiraz was
It could not compare with the open spaces of Ryazan.
Is it because I come from the north?

I'm eager to tell you of a field, Shaganeh
That gave me my rye-colored hair.
Wind a finger around a lock if you wish.
I am oblivious to pain.
I am eager to tell you of a field, Shageneh.

You can guess from my curls, Shaganeh
How moonlight ripples over rye.
Joke with me, sweetheart, and smile.
Just don't awaken my memories
Of moonlight rippling over rye.

Shaganeh, my sweet Shaganeh!
There is a girl in the north like you, Shaganeh.
She looks frighteningly like you, Shaganeh.
Who knows, she may even be thinking of me now …
Shaganeh, my sweet Shaganeh.

Esenin wrote this poem to a young woman he was totally infatuated with, Shaganeh Taliyan. She was an Armenian teacher of Russian language and literature in Batumi. Esenin met her in the winter of 1924-25 when he visited that town. Though he dedicated to her his entire cycle of poems titled "Persian Themes," of which this poem and the following one are a part, his passion was unrequited, though she did love his verses. Five years younger than Esenin, Shaganeh Taliyan died in 1976.

YOU, MY SWEET, SAID THAT SAADI

You, my sweet, said that Saadi
Kissed only on the breast.
For God's sake, give me time.
I'll get it right eventually!

You sang to me: "The roses beyond the Euphrates
Are more lovely than living girls."
If I were a rich man
I'd put it another way.

I'd cut down all those rose bushes
To leave only a single joy …
The joy that no one or nothing
Outshines my sweet Shaganeh.

So stop tormenting me with precepts and vows.
I follow no vows in my life.
I was born a poet
And so shall I kiss like a poet.

Saadi Shirazi was a famous thirteenth-century Persian poet.

YOU DON'T LOVE ME

You don't love me and you don't pity me.
But don't you find me a bit attractive?
You don't look me in the eye but swoon from lust
When you rest your hands on my shoulders.

Young woman, with your sensuous grin
I'll be neither tender nor crude with you.
Tell me how many men you have caressed
How many hands you remember, how many lips.

I know … they've gone, like shadows
Never having touched your flame.
You have sat on many a lap
And now you sit here on mine.

Keep your eyes half shut
And your thoughts on that other man.
I'm not much taken with you.
I sink into distances close to me.

Don't call this fire "fate."
A fling is a frivolity.
I met you entirely by chance
And I'll walk away with a smile on my lips.

And you'll go your own way too
Brushing away joyless days.
Just don't disturb those never kissed.
Don't entice those who never burned.

And when you find yourself strolling with another
On a side street, chatting away about love
Maybe I'll just go for a stroll myself
And meet up with you once again.

You'll lean back further on his shoulder
Lower your gaze a little
And say, calmly, to me, "Good evening."
And I'll reply, "Good evening, Mademoiselle."

Nothing will disturb my soul now.
Nothing will make it tremble.
He who has loved cannot love again.
He who has been burnt to a cinder cannot be re-lit.

THE DAWN IS WEAVING ITS SCARLET LIGHT

The dawn is weaving its scarlet light in the lake.
The wood grouse send their crackling cries through the pines.

An oriole weeps, hidden in some hollow tree.
I'm the only one not crying … I'm full of good cheer.

I know you'll wind your way here at twilight.
We'll sit in a fresh stooked grain sheaf.

I will cover you with kisses, crumple you like a flower.
A man drunk on joy cannot be judged.

You will toss aside your bridal veil under my caresses.
I'll carry you, delirious, to the bushes for the night.

So let the crying of the wood grouse ring out.
There's a cheerful longing in the scarlet threads of dawn.

Once again the mating call of the wood grouse appears, important enough to be mentioned twice. Perhaps "cheerful longing" requires an explanation. Esenin often uses adjectives that seem contradictory to the nouns they modify, and this is one such case. The Russian equivalent of "longing" here is *toska*, one of those nouns that Russians claim as a unique feature of their native disposition. While *toska* is certainly an internally complex word, it has lovely equivalents in English: longing, yearning, melancholy, nostalgia, boredom, ennui, etc. The verbal form can mean "to long for," "to miss," and "to be depressed."

WHAT A NIGHT!

What a night! I can't go on.
I can't sleep. The sky is all moon.
It's as if my heart is still harboring
My youth … my wasted youth.

Lover of those years gone cold
Don't mistake the game for love.
Just let this moonlight stream down
On my propped-up pillow.

Just let that bold light bring out
All my distorted features.
You see, you cannot fall out of love
With someone you have never loved.

You can only love once.
This is why you mean nothing to me:
The linden trees beckon us in vain
With their feet buried in drifts of snow.

You know as well as I know
That in this dark-blue moonlight
Those lindens bear no flowers
Nothing but hoar frost and snow.

You know we fell out of love ages ago
That you didn't love me, and I loved another.
You know, neither of us cared for anything
But the game that passes for love.

Yet despite all this, hold me, caress me
Kiss me with your cunning passion.
And let my heart forever dream of the month of May
And the one I have never ceased to love.

This, one of Esenin's last poems, was apparently written while he was in the clinic, sometime between 26 November and 21 December 1925. It was published posthumously together with the preceding one.

THE FLOWERS SAY FAREWELL TO ME

The flowers say farewell to me
Bowing their heads as low as they can …
That I will never again set eyes on her face
Nor on the place where I was born.

It can't be helped, my darling, it can't!
I've seen them as I have the earth.
And I welcome this funereal shudder
As I do a new-found embrace.

And because I have fully grasped
All life that I passed with a smile
I can say of every passing instant
"Everything on this earth comes back again."

Whatever's happened, there's always another.
Grieving won't soothe the one before.
A new man will write a better song
For a precious woman abandoned.

Yet, when my sweetheart is with her other lover
Rapt in silence with his song
Perhaps she'll think again of me as she would
Of a flower that can only appear once.

COULD I BE THINKING THIS TOO LATE

Could I be thinking this too late or too early?
It's been out of my mind for years and years.
But I've come to resemble Don Juan.
I'm a first-rate frivolous poet.

What's happened? What's going on in me?
Each passing day finds me at some woman's knees.
Each passing day I throw self-pity to the winds
Unrestrained by bitter infidelities.

I have always wished that my heart
Would get less tangled in tender simplicity.
What am I looking for in the eyes of these women
Eyes that are flighty, false and empty?

I wish this scorn of mine would restrain me.
You marked me from the beginning.
And my spirit too is marked
By a frigid seething and the blue rustle of the lilac.

My spirit is branded by the lemon light of sunset
And yet I hear a voice coming through the fog:
"The day of reckoning for unfettered feelings will come.
Be there when it summons you, Don Juan!"

I pick up the gauntlet with a composed mind
And see that I have but one choice …
To revere the blizzard like the dark-blue blooms of May
And call this sensuous trembling "love."

That's what's happened, that's what's going on in me.
That's why I find myself at so many knees.
So that I won't be resigned to bitter betrayal
So that happiness might smile on me forever.

This is another poem, one of his last, published in that February 1926 issue of "Novy Mir."

DON'T TORMENT ME WITH THAT COOLNESS OF YOURS

Don't torment me with that coolness of yours.
And don't ask me how old I am.
A dropping sickness has possessed me.
My soul is a bleached skeleton.

There was a time as a boy in the country
I dreamt of making it to the Big Smoke
That I would someday be rich and famous
And loved by everyone in the land.

Yes! I'm rich, richer than I ever imagined.
I had a top hat, haven't a clue where it's gone.
I'm now the proud owner of a single dickey
And a fashionable pair of worn-out laced boots.

My name is widely recognized
From Moscow to the dregs of Paris.
It inspires terror
Like an obscenity scrawled on a fence.

And love … is there anything more amusing?
You kiss … and your lips are like tin.
My feelings have long since overripened
And yours will never blossom.

It's still too soon for me to mourn.
And if there's sadness, so what?
The fresh saltbush rustles on the barrows
More gold than the gold on your braids.

I'd like nothing more than to be back in that country
Where the fresh saltbush rustles
And to drown forever in obscurity
And dream like a little boy of the Big Smoke …

And to dream of something different and new
Something the earth and the grass cannot grasp
Something the heart cannot express in words
And man does not know what to call.

A LETTER TO A WOMAN

You recall
Of course you recall everything
How I stood
Back against the wall
As you, agitated, paced the room
Hurling blunt words
Into my face.

You said
It was time we parted
That my crazy life
Had worn you out
That you needed to get down to work
Whereas I was only destined
To roll farther into the depths.

Sweetheart!
You didn't love me.
You didn't know that amidst a throng of people
I was like a horse frothing at the mouth
Spurred by a daredevil rider.

You didn't know that I had found myself
Enveloped in a dense fog
In a life lashed by storms.
I was tormented by not fathoming
Where the fate of events was leading us.

You cannot see a person's features
When standing face to face.
You need to step far back to view the big picture.
A ship is in a deplorable state
When the sea's surface is boiling.

Our planet is a ship!
But someone out of the blue
Seeking new life and fresh glory
Has majestically steered her
Straight into the thick of storms and blizzards.

Well, is there one among us who has not fallen
Not cursed and spewed vomit on her main deck?
Few who have experienced life's trials
Remain standing in the violent pitch and roll.

In the pandemonium
Of those times
Fully aware of what I had to do
I too descended into the hold of the ship
So as not to see the spewing on the deck.
As for that hold …
It was a Russian pub.
And, bent over a glass
I lost myself
To drunken delirium
Rather than suffer for anyone.

Darling!
I tormented you.
I saw melancholy
In your tired eyes.
And you saw a show-off
Wasting away in drunken brawls.

You didn't know that I had found myself
Enveloped in a dense fog
In a life lashed by storms.
I was tormented by not fathoming
Where the fate of events was leading us.

* * *

Now years have gone by.
I've grown older.
I'm feeling and thinking things differently.
And when I raise my glass in celebration I say:
"Praise and glory to the man at the helm!"

Today I am in the grip
Of the tenderest feelings.
I recalled you weary and heartbroken.
So at this very moment
I hasten to inform you
About the man I was then
And what has happened to me since.

My love!
It gives me pleasure to tell you
That I escaped a fall from the steepest slope.
I am now the fiercest fellow-traveler
In the land of the Soviets.

I've become a man
Unlike the man I was before.
I wouldn't make you suffer
As I once so often did.
I am prepared to bear the banner of freedom
And joyful toil
Right across Europe to the English Channel!

Forgive me …
You have changed, I know.
You are sharing your life
With a sincere and clever husband.
You don't need any additional pestering.
And you don't need me
Not even one bit.

So live
According to your own stars
Under the cover of an updated net.
Your friend
Who remembers you
Ever yours …
Sergei Esenin.

This poem gives us perhaps the clearest poetic expression of Esenin's "then" – his past – and the "now" – his present state. He was a fellow traveler – a *poputchik* – at a time when this was still an acceptable status to maintain. A neutral term in the years immediately following the revolution, when the Bolsheviks needed all the support they could get, it signified someone who has sympathy with the communist cause but does not join the Party. In Stalin's time, however, which of course Esenin thankfully avoided, this type of individual fell into the category of suspected enemy of the state. The woman to whom Esenin addressed this letter was Zinaida Raikh, his second wife. The "sincere and clever husband" referred to in the poem is Meyerhold, whom she married in 1922, the year after her marriage to Esenin ended in divorce.

"Joyful toil" comes across as a cliché in English, and this is the sound it should have, as the original Russian phrase, *svetlyi trud*, seems purposely hackneyed. Esenin's attempt at banner running comes across as halfhearted, certainly lacking in the energy it would take to get from Russia to the English Channel on one's own steam.

DON'T REPROACH ME WITH THOSE LOOKS OF YOURS

Don't reproach me with those looks of yours.
I nurse no disdain for you.
I do love your listless and languishing eyes
Not to mention your cunning meekness.

You seem to welcome me with open arms
And it gladdens my heart to see
How a vixen, while feigning death
Catches ravens and their little chicks.

Catch me if you can, I won't be craven.
But what if your passion's died out?
Such women have often been burned
On my bitterly cold heart.

It's not you I love, my sweetheart.
You are but an echo and a shadow.
I see the dream of another in your face.
Her eyes are a light-blue domain.

She may not look as meek and mild as you
And, well, she does come across as cold.
But when she walks, her majestic figure
Stirs me to the bone.

It's hard not to be faithful to her.
She draws you to her whether you like it or not.
While, as for you, there's no place in my heart
For your sweet and rapturous lies.

While, all in all, I do repudiate you
I'm embarrassed and troubled to say:
"If there were no heaven and no hell
Man would have invented one in the end."

Esenin entered the psychiatric clinic under the supervision of Prof. Pyotr Gannushkin, an eminent psychiatrist of his day. The poet was, in a word, suicidal. Alcohol had ravaged his reason and he was in despair at the way the new Soviet reality was destroying his beloved old Russia. He feared, not without grounds, that his poetry would be censored and, at worst, forgotten. To make matters worse, his recent marriage to Sofia Tolstaya was by no means a happy one. This is yet another in the group of amazing poems published in "Novy Mir" in February 1926.

I WANDER OVER THE FIRST SNOW

I wander over the first snow
With lilies-of-the-valley exploding in my heart.
The evening has lit up a star over my path
With its dark-blue candle.

I can't tell if this is the light or the dark …
If it's the wind or a rooster singing in the woods.
Maybe it's not winter on the fields at all
But swans who've set down in the meadow.

Oh white satin, how good you are!
This light frost warms my blood!
I feel the urge to press the naked breasts
Of the birch to my body.

Ah, this thick forest mist!
Ah, the joy of these snowbound fields!
I feel the urge to enfold my arms
Around the willow's wooden thighs.

This is one of Esenin's most explicitly sensuous poems focusing on nature. It is wholly Russian nature that he is so passionately enamored of. It was published in September 1918 in the newspaper "Evening News of the Moscow Soviet." I wonder how the workers, just a year into the revolution, related to its erotic animism.

DEAR LEAFLESS MAPLE

Dear leafless maple, blanketed in ice
Why are you bending to this blizzard?

Have you glimpsed something? Overheard something?
It's as if you left the village on a binge.

And out on the road like a drunken watchman
Your leg froze stiff, trapped in a snowdrift.

Oh, I too now stand on shaky ground.
I've lost my way while carousing about.

I've bumped into pussy willows, bowed to pines
Serenading them in blizzards with the songs of summer.

I've envisaged myself as a maple like you
Though not a bare one, but one green all over.

And, modesty to the winds, as thick as a plank
I've caressed a birch tree, like another man's wife.

Esenin wrote this poem while at the psychiatric clinic in November 1925. His room was on the second floor overlooking the garden.

TO KACHALOV'S DOG

Come on, Jim, give me your paw for good luck.
I've never seen a paw to match it.
Let's bark at the moon together.
Let's bark at this calm noiseless sky.
Come on, Jim, give me your paw for good luck.

Please, buddy, don't lick me like that.
You've got to understand the simple truth
'Cause you've no idea what life is
What it means to live in this world.

Your owner is kind, a celebrity
And his home is always crawling with guests.
And they all grin and reach out to you
To stroke your velvety fur.

You're fiendishly handsome as dogs go
And you have a sweet trusting nature.
And selfless creature that you are
You slobber your kisses like a drunken pal.

My dear old Jim, there've been all sorts
Who've come as guests to your home.
But by any chance has she been among them
The one more sorrowful and silent than all the rest?

She'll come, let's shake on it.
Give her one of your constant stares.
Lick her hand tenderly for me in my absence
For all my sins, real or imagined.

The owner of the dog was the very famous actor and friend of Esenin, Vasily Kachalov (1875-1948). Kachalov worked under Konstantin Stanislavsky at the Moscow Art Theater.

POEM ABOUT A DOG

In the morning, in the barn for rye
Where bast mats stand in golden rows
She gave birth to a litter of seven
Seven chestnut-color pups.

She fondled them until the evening came
Licking them all over
As the snow melted into trickles
Under the warmth of her belly.

But in the evening, when the hens
Sit restfully on their perches
The grim master appeared
And dropped all seven puppies into a sack.

The mother raced over the snowdrifts
Not letting the master get ahead.
And for ages the smooth surface of water
Unfrozen, would not cease its trembling.

And when, in the end, she dragged herself back
Licking the moisture off her flanks
She took the moon, shining over the shack
For one of her puppies.

She gazed up into the dark blue sky
Whining for all she was worth.
But the thin moon slipped behind a hill
Disappearing beyond the fields.

And just as when they mock her
By tossing a stone at her instead of food
Her eyes rolled silently
Like golden stars into the snow.

This translation is dedicated to Gabriella Page-Fort.

This poem is based on a real incident, in which a neighbor of the Esenins in his boyhood village killed an entire litter of puppies.

SON OF A BITCH

Once again the years have swum out of the dark
Rustling like a field of moon daisies.
It all takes me back to a dog I once knew
The friend of my younger days.

Now my youth has lost its voice
Like the garden maple rotting from its roots.
But I can't forget the girl in white and the dog
Who delivered my letters to her.

Not everyone has someone they love
But this girl was like a song to me.
She never touched the letters I sent
Slipped under the collar of the dog.

She never read a single one of them.
She never came to know my writing.
All she did was dream and dream
By the wayfaring tree at the yellow pond.

I suffered … I longed for a reply …
I couldn't wait … I left … and now
After years … I'm back home again …
The famous poet at his village gates.

That dog has long since given up the ghost.
But her young son has now rushed to meet me.
He has a coat of her color, blue sheen
And the very same mad yelp.

Oh mother and son, how you're alike!
It's evoked all the old pain in my heart.
This pain has somehow made me young enough
To pen those notes to her again.

I'd gladly hear that old song again.
But don't bark! Just don't bark! Don't!
Do you want me to kiss you, my canine friend
For reawakening May in my heart?

I will kiss you and press my body against you
And take you as a friend into my house.
Yes, I did once fall for a girl in white.
But now it's the blue one I love.

This poem was written in 1924 and published in "Novy Mir" in March 1925.

The title in Russian has, as it does in English, both the literal meaning of "male puppy" and the figurative slang meaning.

A LETTER TO MY MOTHER

Are you still alive, my old Mum?
I am too. Greetings to you. Greetings!
May that inexpressible evening light
Stream over your little cottage.

They write me that you fret over me
Keeping your anxieties to yourself
That you often come out on to the road
In your tattered old-fashioned little smock.

They say that, in the dark blue of evening
A single image haunts you
That someone in a barroom brawl
Has rammed a hunting knife beneath my heart.

It's nothing, dearest, do not fret.
It's someone's bitter ravings.
I'm not such a hopeless drunkard
That I'd die without seeing you again.

I'm still the tender boy I was before
And dream of one thing only
To get out of this rebellious tedium
Back to our poor little house.

I'll be back when the spring stretches
Branches throughout our whitened garden.
Only, don't wake me up at dawn
Like you used to eight years ago.

Don't awaken dreams too old to dream.
Don't stir a hope that never came true.
Fate put me to the test of loss
And weariness long before my time.

And don't teach me prayers. Just don't!
There's no going back to the past.
You alone are my comfort and consolation.
You alone are my inexpressible light.

So, forget all that worry of yours.
Don't yearn so longingly for me.
Don't come out on to the road so often
In your tattered old-fashioned little smock.

THE SNOW SPLITS AND SHATTERS

The snow splits and shatters
Below a shivering radiant moon.
Once again I catch sight of the village fence
And, through the blizzard, a window light.

We are all homeless, but we don't need much.
I sing about what's been given to me.
So tonight I'm back at the family table
And once again my old Mum's before me.

She looks at me with tear-filled eyes
Calmly, silently, as if not distressed.
I looked at her transfixed
As the teacup just slid from her fingers.

Sweet, good-hearted, old, tender Mum!
Banish every sad thought from your mind.
Listen to me … I'll tell you of my life
To the sound of this harmonica snow.

I've seen much of life. I've roamed.
I've loved to death and suffered my share.
The reason why I've caroused and rioted …
Is that I've never found anyone better than you.

Now again I'm warmed by the stove
My shoes and jacket flung aside.
Once again I've come through and once again I hope
To recapture the light that was my childhood.

The blizzard whimpers outside my window
A haze of wild noise.
And I picture linden flowers scattering …
White throughout our garden.

SING ME THAT SONG

Sing me that song, the one our old mum
Sang to us a long time ago.
I'll manage to sing along with you
Without regretting hope long gone.

I know the tune and words so well
So let's hear it, wind me up, alarm me.
It's as if I'm hearing once again
The tender tremor in her voice.

So come on and sing it for me
And I'll lightly shut my eyes
And I'll sing along with you and see again
The familiar features of her face.

Sing for me. You see, I'm pleased.
I'm not the only one who ever loved
The garden gate in autumn
And the rowan leaves falling to earth.

Sing for me, will you, then I'll recall.
I won't forget myself and brood.
It gives me pleasure and lightens me up
To see Mother and her brooding hens.

I fell for the young birch's figure
For the fogs and the dew around.
I fell in love with her golden braids
And her hessian sarafans.

And that's why my heart is so light now
Thanks to your song and this wine ...
Because you seemed to me like the little birch tree
That stands by our window at home.

The subject of this poem and the following one is Esenin's sister Alexandra (1911-1981). She left Konstantinovo in the autumn of 1924 to continue her studies in Moscow, where her brother was living. In the dedication of this poem he refers to her by a nickname, Shura; but he used other diminutives of her name, such as Shurenok and Shurevna, to show his affection for her. She wrote in her memoir published decades after her brother's death that he had always treated her tenderly. He dedicated four poems in all to her, of which I have chosen two.

One early September's day in 1925, Esenin and his soon-to-be wife Sofia took Shura on a carriage ride. They went to a restaurant. It was the young country girl's first time to dine out. She wore a colorful country shawl, a *platok*, which is often translated as "handkerchief"; yet these garments were large and draped over the shoulder. Her brother remarked to her how beautiful she was, despite her embarrassment and shyness. The next day he wrote "I've Never Seen Women As Lovely As You," dedicating it to her.

Incidentally, Alexandra married journalist Pyotr Ilyin in May 1929. They had three children and stayed together their whole life.

I'VE NEVER SEEN WOMEN AS LOVELY AS YOU

I've never seen women as lovely as you.
Yet, you know, I am harboring in my heart
A certain resentment, not necessarily bitter
That you are reliving my youth.

You are my cornflower-blue word
And I will love you forever and ever.
How is our cow getting along these days?
Still tugging at its sorry straw?

I do love it when you sing to me.
Heal me with a childhood dream.
Has our rowan tree lost its fire
Strewing its berries below our white window?

What does Mother sing while dressing flax?
I turned my back on the village forever.
But I want you to know … a crimson blizzard
Has littered our porch with leaves.

I know that the dog we left behind
The one who now gets no fondling or tears
Is quietly whimpering for us by the gate
As one mourns a bride who's gone.

Yet there's no need to return to it all
For it came to me out of time—
Your beautiful shawl from Ryazan
Like heartache, like rapture, like love.

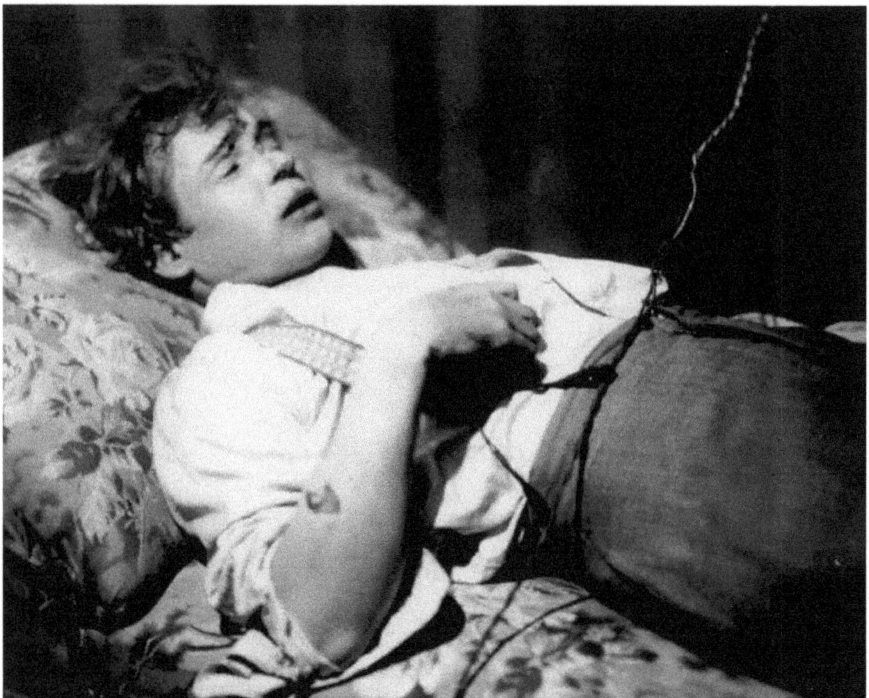

PART FOUR

The Bitter End

It's a dangerous exercise to psychoanalyze famous figures from the past. Anyone who has encountered depression knows how hard it is to determine the true nature of a mood disorder. But perhaps in Esenin's case it is not impossible. It was recognized by everyone in his inner circle of friends that he suffered from severe alcoholism and depression. He recognized and admitted this as well. He could control neither his alcoholism nor his wild mood swings. Friends knew him as a reticent man, a kind and considerate listener. Then, suddenly, generally as the result of the consumption of alcohol, he would break into an abusive attack on those around him, producing one after another example from the vast and colorful storehouse of Russian-language swearwords, before, as often as not, dissolving into tears and sobs. Toward the end, friends were afraid to leave him alone. He too was terrified of what he might do to himself.

Novelist Yuri Olesha (1899-1960), author of that remarkable novel *Envy*, described a night with Esenin and a few others, including Ilya Ilf (1897-1937), one of the duo who wrote brilliant comic novels still popular in Russia today. Esenin arrived looking a mess in dinner jacket and patent leather shoes. He had obviously been in a fight with somebody. Though he was drunk he started to recite "The Man in Black." He reached out to grasp a bookcase but it came crashing down to the floor.

Novelist Valentin Kataev (1897-1986) was also there and described how erratic his recitation was, hollering some lines while saying others in a whisper so soft as to be inaudible.

On 27 November 1925, Esenin wrote one of his last letters, this one to Pyotr Chagin (1898-1967), friend and supporter, who as editor of the "Baku Worker" published Esenin's poems …

"Dear Pyotr! I'm writing to you from the hospital in bed again. Why—I don't know, but no one probably knows. You see, my nerves have to be treated…. The theory is that walls treat one more effectively than any medicine. … I'm sending you 'The Man in Black.' Read it and think about how we struggle, lying in bed."

I said that Esenin was aware of how ill he was, though the letter to Pyotr Chagin suggests ignorance or denial. In actuality, as many of us do, he vacillated between objective self-knowledge and optimistic delusion.

Had he come to see his mental affliction, exacerbated by alcohol, as the sine qua non of creative genius? He also wrote this …

"…The deaf Beethoven is superior to a less talented Rubenstein who can hear, and a drunk Edgar Poe is more wonderful than a sober Mark Krinitsky…."

Was he excusing his affliction and excesses as states concomitant with the creative process, as qualities, if you will, that make self-pity justifiable? (Mark Krinitsky (1874-1952), by the way, was the pen name of Mikhail Samygin, a Russian author who, by coincidence, had taught at a Ryazan school. He too, alas, succumbed to depression in the 1930s and passed away in a mental health facility.)

Esenin's visits to the Caucasus in 1924 and 1925 had invigorated him, and his infatuation with the exotic scenes and women there is evidence enough of this. By mid-1925 he genuinely felt that he could conquer his alcohol addiction and the image of himself as a rowdy and uncouth youth. Everything now, he wrote, "is going to be different." But the "the man in black" won.

Anna Izryadnova met him for the last time on 23 December 1925, a few days before his death. She said that he begged for forgiveness, and when she asked him why, he just told her he was going away, "no doubt to die."

He escaped from the clinic in Moscow, went to Leningrad and checked into a hotel. On the morning of 28 December his body and his final poem (see page 187) were discovered in the room. The photograph at the top of this part was taken that morning in Room No. 5 at the Hotel Angleterre on the corner of Voznesensky Prospekt and Malaya Morskaya Street in the center of the city that was then called Leningrad. (Only the façade is original today; and the reconstructed hotel behind it is part of the Hotel Astoria complex.)

His death shook Russia … and, in some ways, continues to. Even in recent years conspiracy theories have circulated, Russia being The Motherland of Conspiracy Theories, where the conspiracy theory becomes news even before news is allowed to happen. That Esenin's escape from the clinic was aided by a Chekist mole; that he was murdered, and the gash on his forehead was the result of being struck by a blunt object; that he couldn't have written his last poem in his own blood because the quantity coming from his cut finger would not have been sufficient; that he wouldn't have cut a finger on his right hand, which was his good hand, if he was going to write with it….

I certainly have no idea how much of this bears truth. But what is certain is that virulent public attacks on Esenin and his poetry were the order of the day after his death. RAPP, the Russian Association of Proletarian Writers, an organization that had come into being at the beginning of 1925, called him "a banner of kulak counterrevolution." (*Kulak*, meaning "fist," for their alleged tight grip on grain, was a derogatory term for any peasant or farmer who resisted the collectivization of agriculture.) Member of the Politburo Nikolai Bukharin (1888-1938), though a relative moderate when it came to treatment of people in the countryside, condemned what he called "Eseninism" in the strongest terms.

At Esenin's funeral, which was a civil service, the coffin rested in the House of Printing on Nikitsky Boulevard. Kachalov (see page 135) read, and renowned operatic tenor Leonid Sobinov (1872-1934) sang. Zinaida Raikh attended with her children. She cried out, "Our sun has gone away!" Meyerhold was there to comfort her. Esenin's mother stood gazing around at all the people who were so different from the people she knew back home.

To say that a great deal has changed in Russia in the past century is to state the obvious. I would not claim that to know Russia you should read the poetry of Sergei Esenin.

But I would say that if you want to know how Russians feel about their country, read the poetry of Sergei Esenin. That "old plank bridge" spans not only eras but centuries; and not only one Russia with another, but Russia with the rest of the world.

WE ARE ON OUR WAY NOW

We are on our way now step by step
To that land of tranquility and bliss.
It might be time for me as well
To pack my slight worldly goods for the journey.

Oh my beloved birchwood forests!
And you, the earth, and you, the sands of the plains!
I haven't the strength to hide my grief
Before the host of departing souls.

In this world I have loved too much
All that envelops the spirit in flesh.
Peace to the aspens who've hurled their branches
And peered into rose-color waters.

I have mulled over many thoughts in silence.
I have composed many poems about myself.
And I am happy that I lived and breathed
On this, our gloomy earth.

I am happy that I have kissed my women
Lolled about the grass, crumpling flowers
And that I never struck a single animal
Our little brothers, over the head.

I know that groves don't bloom there
And that rye stalks don't jangle like swan necks.
That is why I shudder ceaselessly
Before the host of departing souls.

I know that in that land you won't find
Cornfields like gilded shadows.
That is why I love my fellow man …
Because he lives with me on this earth.

The prompt for writing this poem was the sudden death, from meningitis, of Esenin's close friend Alexander Shirayevets on 15 May 1924. Shirayevets had been one of the earliest admirers of Esenin's poetry, telling him as much in 1915. Esenin was bereft with grief at the loss of his friend.

A DARK-BLUE FOG

A dark-blue fog. A wide expanse of snow
And thin lemon lunar light.
My heart aches with a quiet pleasure
As my mind wanders back to my early years.

The snow by the porch was like shifting sand.
I had pulled down my cat-fur cap back to front
And, without a word, snuck away from home
By the light of just such a moon.

Now I've come back to the place of my birth.
Who remembers me? Who's forgotten?
It grieves me to be the persecuted wanderer
Now the not-so-young lord of his own hut.

I quietly crumple my new cap.
Sable fur's not my thing.
I recall grandpa, I recall grandma
I recall the loose snow on churchyard graves.

All are at peace now … we'll all be there too
Whatever precautions we take.
And that's why I am drawn to people.
That's why I love people on this earth.

That explains the tears welling in my eyes
And the smile on my lips as I snuff out my light …
As if I am seeing for the very last time
This hut with the dog on its porch.

THAT'S IT! IT'S SET

That's it! It's set … there's no getting back.
I've left the fields of home for good.
No longer now will the poplars ring
Their whirling leaves above my head.

My home will stoop lower without me.
My old dog is long since dead.
It's on the buckled streets of Moscow
That God has fated me, I know, to die.

I love this elmed city
Even if she is flabby and decrepit.
Drowsy golden Asia has lain down to sleep
Atop her cupolas and domes.

And when at night the moon comes out
How it shines! … God only knows how!
I hang my head and take a walk
Down an alley to my old pub.

There's a din and racket in that infernal place.
But I spend the night there till dawn
Reciting my poems to the prostitutes
And burning through liquor with crooks.

My heart beats faster and faster
And I can no longer control my words …
"I, like you, have fallen
And there's no way for me to get back."

My home will stoop lower without me.
My old dog is long since dead.
It's on the buckled streets of Moscow
That God has fated me, I know, to die.

WE ARE ALL MARKED

We are all marked in our own special way
From the very first days of our lives.
If I'd not been a poet
I would no doubt have been a swindler and a thief.

All skin and bones and by no means tall
I was always the hero among the lads
Often making my way home
With a smashed-up nose.

I'd mutter to my terrified mum
Through lips caked in blood:
"Forget it! I just tripped over a stone.
I'll be as good as new in the morning."

And now, when the scalding mold of those days
Has, in fact, gone cold
That restless insolent force of long ago
Has spilled over into my poems.

Now it's a cluster of golden words
Reflecting my old bravado
In every incessant line
The bravado of the bully and brat.

I'm just as brave and proud as I was then
But with a new spring in my step …
If they once smashed me in the mug
They're now bloodying my soul.

So now I say not to my mum
But to the guffawing rabble of strangers:
"Forget it! I just tripped over a stone.
I'll be as good as new in the morning."

A profound self-knowledge, if mixed with a somewhat maudlin self-pity, pervades Esenin's poetry. Given his deep mood swings, he does try to put a brave face on his encounters with the fists and arrows of his detractors and enemies.

THE MAN IN BLACK

Friend, my friend
I am sick, very sick.
I've no idea where this pain has sprung from.
Is it the wind whistling
Over a desolate and deserted field?
Or is it the liquor that strips my brain bare
Branches in a September woodland.

My head is flapping its ears
As a bird does its wings.
Its foot, my neck
Is numb to signals.
The man in black
Black, black
The man in black
Has sat beside me on the bed
This man in black
Keeping me awake throughout the night.

The man in black
Fingers his foul book
And intoning through his nose
Like a monk chanting over a dead body
He recites to me the book of the life
Of some drunken scoundrel
Striking depression and dread into my soul.
The man in black
Black, black!

"Listen to me, listen"
He mutters to me.
"There is a host of the most beautiful
Ideas and plans in this book.
There was a man
Who lived his life in a country
Groaning with the most revolting
Thugs and charlatans.

The December snow in that country
Is fiendishly white
And the blizzards whirl
Light-hearted spinning wheels.
The man was an adventurer
Who on his own
Reached the highest heights.

He was the picture of elegance
And a poet to boot.
His powers were limited
But adequate.
And he fell for some woman
Age forty-plus
Whom he called his vulgar little girl
And sweetheart.

Happiness," he went on
"Is in an agile wit and touch.
The souls who lack such agility
Are destined to be miserable.
Who cares
That so much suffering
Is brought about by perverted
Two-timing gestures?

When storms thunder and rage
When freezing cold bites your days
When you grieve
Under the heaviest losses
To put on a smile and appear simple
Is the highest form of artistic expression in the world."

"Man in black!
What gives you the right?!
You're not some professional
Lifeguard.
I couldn't care less about the life
Of some lout of a poet.
Please recite your story
To somebody else."

The man in black
Peers straight into my eyes.
His eyes are filmed
With light-blue vomit.
It's as if he's trying to tell me
That I'm a crook, a thief
Who has fleeced someone
Brazenly and shamelessly.

* * *

Friend, my friend
I am sick, very sick.
I've no idea where this pain has sprung from.
Is it the wind whistling
Over a desolate and deserted field?
Or is it the liquor that strips my brain bare
Branches in a September woodland.

The night is freezing.
It is still at the crossroads.
I sit by myself by the window sill
Expecting neither guest nor friend.
A soft blanket of crumbling quicklime
Covers the entire plain.
And the trees have assembled in our garden
Like men on horseback.

A night bird cries out somewhere
Its evil tidings.
The wooden horsemen
Sow clattering hooves.
And again that man in black
Is sitting down in my easy chair
Having tipped his top hat
And casually flung open his frock coat.

"Listen to me, listen!"
He wheezes, looking me straight in the face.
And he leans closer
Right up to me.
"I've never seen anyone
Out of all the villains I know
Who's suffered from insomnia
As pointlessly and absurdly as you.

Ah, let's say I'm mistaken.
I mean, just look at that moon!
What more does the world need
To give itself over to a drunken slumber?
Maybe that woman with her fleshy thighs
Will steal in here
And you'll recite to her
Your languorous sickly verse.

Oh, I just adore poets!
They're such an amusing lot.
I always find stories in them
I've heard time and again.
They're all about some long-haired freak
Telling a pimply schoolgirl about the world
When all he wants
Is to get into her pants.

I don't know, I can't recall …
But there lived a boy
Of simple peasant stock
In a village
Maybe Kaluga
Or maybe Ryazan.
He was blond
With pale-blue eyes …

And when he grew up
He turned into a poet.
His powers were limited
But adequate.
And he fell for some woman
Age forty-plus
Whom he called his vulgar little girl
And sweetheart."

"Man in black!
You are a vile and revolting guest.
And that reputation has preceded you
For ages."
I am fit to be tied, seething.
I bring my walking stick
Down on his mug
Right over the bridge of his nose …

* * *

… The moon has perished.
The dark-blue dawn strikes my little window.
Oh you, the night!
You, the night, what have you been digging up?
I stand here in a top hat.
There is no one with me.
I am all by myself …
In front of a shattered mirror….

Esenin was quick to remark to friends that the reference to "the man in black" came from Pushkin. In 1830 Pushkin wrote a short play, the second of his "little tragedies," titled *Mozart and Salieri*. In Act Two, Mozart senses that he is being haunted by a man in black who, he believes, is sitting at his very table. He says to Salieri, "Genius and villainy are two things that do not go hand in hand, don't you think?" Esenin was clearly identifying with Mozart (and Pushkin!) and saw himself surrounded by poetic Salieris.

A friend once caught Esenin standing before a mirror, grimacing and talking to himself.

And there was another witness to the fact that this man in black had come to haunt him. It was the actress Avgusta Mikhlashevskaya (see pg. 91 in Loves), who wrote, many years after Esenin's death, about her last meeting with him toward the end of 1925. They had gone with some others to a dacha outside Moscow. Esenin stood up in a room with a low ceiling and read "The Man in Black." She became terrified. It was as if Esenin didn't see anyone in the room except a man in black beside him.

NO ONE CAN DISPEL THIS SORROW

No one can dispel this sorrow
With peals of laughter from years gone by.
The white flowers on my linden are spent.
The nightingale dawn has stilled.

Everything was new to me once.
My heart was bursting with feelings.
But now even a tender word slips from my lips
Like bitter fruit.

The vast moonlit plains once so familiar
Do nothing for me now.
The pits … the tree stumps … the tips of debris
Now only dispirit this Russian landscape.

The sick, the feeble, the low …
A gray smooth waterscape …
I weep the moment I recall
All the things native and dear to me.

The little leaning hut
The bleating of the sheep, the old horse
Who waves her withered tail to the wind
While gazing into the cheerless pond.

This is all that we call our homeland.
This is why people drink
And shed tears with the rains
Hoping for them to clear
Waiting for days that will smile on them.

This is why no one can dispel this sorrow
With peals of laughter from years gone by.
The white flowers on my linden are spent.
The nightingale dawn has stilled.

FAREWELL, BAKU!

Farewell, Baku! I won't see you again.
Deep down I feel sorrow, deep down I feel fear.
My heart below my hand feels closer, tighter
And I feel the power of that simple word: friend.

Farewell, Baku! Farewell, deep blue Turkic sky!
My blood runs colder and my powers are weaker.
But I will take to my grave the bliss
Of a Balaxani May and the waves on the Caspian Sea.

Farewell, Baku! Farewell to you, simple song!
I embrace you, a friend, for the very last time …
May your head nod tenderly to me
Like a golden rose in a lilac haze.

Esenin visited Baku in April/May 1925 and fell seriously ill there. He suspected tuberculosis, but it turned out to be a bad cold. This is when he witnessed the May First celebrations that he wrote about in the poem of that title.

The famous Azerbaijani baritone, a cult figure in his own country and Russia, once dubbed the "Soviet Sinatra," Muslim Mahammad oglu Magomayev, composed beautiful music to this poem.

FOOLISH HEART

Foolish heart, stop your throbbing!
We are all deluded by happiness.
A beggar begs only for sympathy …
Foolish heart, stop your throbbing.

The yellow charms of the moon
Flow over the chestnut trees into the meadows.
I will bow before Lala's shalwars
And take refuge under her chador.
Foolish heart, stop your throbbing.

We have all been known like children
To have our laughter turned to tears.
We've all had our full share
Of joys and of failures.
Foolish heart, stop your throbbing.

I've seen many countries in my day
And looked for happiness wherever I went.
But I will no longer continue to seek
My most wished-for fate.
Foolish heart, stop your throbbing.

Life has not entirely deluded us.
We can still drink our fill of new strength.
And you, my heart, can simply fall asleep
Here … in your lover's lap.
Life has not entirely deluded us.

And perhaps destiny itself will take note of us
As its avalanche streams on by.
And perhaps it will answer love
With a nightingale's song.
Foolish heart, stop your throbbing.

Shalwars are similar to pantaloons.

AH, YOU SLEIGHS!

Ah, you sleighs! And horses, horses!
It's clear that the Devil put you here on Earth.
Your little bells laugh till they weep
As you speed headlong over the steppe.

No moon shines and no dog barks
For as far as the eye can see.
Hold on tight, my dashing life!
I've still got years to go.

Sing out, old driver, in defiance of this night!
I'll sing along, if you wish
Of a young girl's wily eyes
And of my own ecstatic youth.

Ah, I used to cock my hat
Harness the horses to the sleigh
Then lie down on an armful of straw.
Think back to what everyone called me.

I swaggered about as I pleased.
And I won the heart of many a girl
With my concertina conversing
Through the midnight quiet.

That's all history. My hair's thinned out.
The horse has expired, our yard's deserted.
The concertina has lost its voice
Forgotten how to hold a conversation.

But my spirit has not gone cold
And I still feel at home in the snow and the frost.
And that's why the sleigh bells still laugh till they weep
Over all in my life that once was.

I'LL STOP DECEIVING MYSELF

I'll stop deceiving myself.
My gloomy heart is weighed down by cares.
Why am I seen as a charlatan?
Why am I considered a lout?

I'm no villain or highwayman
And I've never shot poor men in dungeons.
I'm just a street playboy
With a ready smile for everyone I meet.

I'm simply a fun-loving, artful Moscovite.
And every dog on every corner
In the districts of downtown
Can tell me by the lightness of my step.

Every clapped-out horse
Greets me with a nod.
I'm a loyal friend to all animals.
My poems are balm to their souls.

The top hat I wear is not for the ladies.
I don't have the strength to entertain foolish passions.
It diminishes my sorrow, and it's easier
To feed a mare golden oats from it.

I'm not up to being friends with people.
I've submitted myself to a different kind of realm.
I'm always ready to give my best necktie
To the first stud who comes along.

I'll stop myself from agonizing over things.
The dark whirlpool has lulled in my gloomy heart.
That's why I'm considered a charlatan.
That's why I'm seen as a lout.

LITTLE HOUSE WITH YOUR SKY-BLUE SHUTTERS

Little house with your sky-blue shutters
You will never leave my mind.
The years that echoed in the dusk
Stayed all too close to me.

I still dream today
Of our fields, our meadow and woods
With the pale-gray calico of our poor northern skies
Drawn lightly over them.

I'm long past being enchanted
And don't fancy losing myself in the wilds.
But I'll probably possess forever
The tender grief of the Russian mind.

I've come to love the gray cranes
Flying with fluty calls into the thin distance
Unable to find enough grain for themselves
In the expanse of plain below.

But they've seen the flowering birches
And the broom bushes, leafless and gnarled
And they've heard the whistles of robbers
That can send a man soon to his grave.

However much I'd like not to love you
I still cannot learn how to do it …
But I cherish you, my native village
Lying beneath your cheap calico.

And though the years of youth no longer
Linger in the air
You will never leave my mind, not ever
Little house with your sky-blue shutters.

Esenin published this poem in September 1924 in "Novy Mir." He often uses words from the rural dialect of his native region, and one found in this poem is *vyt*. A vyt is a measure of land that in Konstantinovo corresponded to fifty to sixty homesteads. Fields and pastures were parceled out according to this measure. The adjective modifying this word here is *rodimaya*, or native. I chose to use "village" rather than get involved with complicated measures that would, in all likelihood, disturb the poem's flow.

THE PLAINS ARE BLANKETED IN SNOW

The plains are blanketed in snow, the moon is white.
A shroud has descended over the landscape.
Birch trees in white weep in the forests.
Who perished here? Who's died? Could it be me myself?

THERE'S ONLY ONE AMUSING PASTIME LEFT FOR ME

There's only one amusing pastime left for me:
To slip my fingers into my mouth and catcall.
There's a vicious rumor going around
That I'm a lout and a foul-mouthed brawler.

Ah, what a laughable loss that is
Even among life's innumerable laughable losses!
I'm ashamed of myself that I once believed in God.
And I'm bitter now that I no longer believe.

Everything beyond the horizon is gold.
The gloom of life's routine extinguishes all else.
I became a lout and a foul-mouthed brawler
Just to burn as brightly as I could.

A poet has a gift for caressing and scribbling
And his fate is all but sealed.
I longed to tie the nuptial knot
Between a white rose and a black toad.

I don't care if those rose-colored wishes
Ever saw the light of day.
If devils have nested in my soul
It means that angels once lived there too.

Now for some merriment in my gloom
As I set out with it for a distant land.
At this very last minute I want
To ask all those who'll be with me …

… That for all my burdensome sins
And for my disbelief in God's grace …
To lay me out in a Russian rubashka
To breathe my last beneath the icons.

I'VE POISONED YOU WITH A BITTER POISON

I've poisoned you with a bitter poison
Young years of loudmouth glory.

I don't know … is my end near or far away?
Eyes that were once deep blue are now pale clouds.

Where are you, delight, in this darkness, horror, grief, abuse?
Are you out in the field? In the pub? I can't see a thing.

I stretch out my hands to feel the way …
We ride … a sleigh … horses … snow … through a wood.

"Hey, driver, use your whip! What are you made of, eh?
You can't lose your soul to a few bumps and potholes!"

The driver comes back, "You'll be lost, my friend
If the horses foam up in a snowstorm like this."

"You, driver, are a wimp! We'll never get anywhere this way!"
So I grabbed the knout and cracked it on the horses' backs.

I lash out … and the horses whirl through a blizzard of snowflakes.
The sleigh jolts … and I go flying straight into a snowdrift.

The next thing I know, what the hell, I'm not in a flying troika
But in a hospital bed bandaged up to my eyeballs.

No longer lashing horses on a bumpy road
I'm lashed myself with soggy lint on a stiff bed.

The hands on the face of the clock twirl like moustaches
As sleepy nurses lean far over me.

And as they lean they shriek, "Oh you golden-haired boy
You've poisoned yourself with a bitter poison.

We don't know if your end is near or far away …
But it is liquor that clouded your deep-blue eyes."

Esenin recited this poem to a friend while convalescing in the hospital in March 1924. The friend, literary scholar and journalist Sofia Vinogradskaya (1901-1964), published a memoir titled *How Esenin Lived* less than a year after his death. She wrote about the bedside reading in her book …

"He not so much read the poem as wheezed it out, straining with all his might in his sickbed to which he was chained, beating the hard bed with his bandaged hand. Before us was not a poet reading his poems but a man who was narrating the brutal truth of his life, a man who was screaming out about his agonies. … When he finished, exhausted, he sunk down into his pillow, put his hand on his face and over his hair and said, 'This is just such an insignificant and worthless little poem.' "

YOU, MY LAND, MY NATIVE LAND

You, my land, my native land
With your tinny autumn rains!
The frozen street lamp reflects
Its lipless head in a black puddle.

No, it's better for me not to look
Lest I suddenly see something worse.
I'll just squint my eyes at the sight
Of all this dismal rust.

It's a bit warmer and less painful that way.
Look! Between skeletons of houses
The belfry bears copper sacks of bells
Like a miller.

If you are hungry, you will be fed with good things …
If unhappy, you'll find yourself filled with joy.
Just do not look at things with wide-open eyes
My dear and unknown earthly brother.

I've acted as I intended to act.
But, alas, this changed absolutely nothing.
My body has obviously become too accustomed
To sensations of shivering cold.

So what of it? There are many others like me
Living and breathing in this world.
The street lamp keeps blinking and howling with laughter
Through the lipless mouth on its head.

Only my heart under its threadbare clothing
Whispers to me, a visitor on this earth:
"Death alone, my friend, will shut the lids
Over eyes that have seen the light."

The reference to "fed with good things" is from Luke 1:53: He hath filled the hungry with good things; and the rich he hath sent empty away.

GOODBYE, MY FRIEND, FAREWELL

Goodbye, my friend, farewell.
You are so close as to be in my heart.
While we are destined to part now
Our reunion is promised ahead.

Goodbye, my friend, not a hand, not a word …
Let neither grief nor sorrow cloud your eyes.
It's a very old thing in life to die
And, of course, nothing new to live.

This is Esenin's final poem, which he wrote using his blood for ink before he ended his life by hanging himself from the ceiling's heating pipes in his hotel room.

SERGEI ALEXANDROVICH ESENIN

A Chronology

He is born on 3 October 1895 in the village of Konstantinovo, some forty-odd kilometers from the provincial city of Ryazan.

His sister Ekaterina is born on 22 November 1905.

In 1909 he completes four years of study at a local school, transferring to a church-affiliated school in the nearby town of Spas-Klepiki.

His sister Alexandra is born on 16 March 1911.

In 1912 he finishes his studies in Spas-Klepiki and in July, age sixteen, he leaves home for Moscow.

In March 1913 he is working at a printers' while writing poetry; and in September he enrolls in the historical-philosophy department at the A. L. Shanyavsky Moscow City Open University. He marries Anna Izryadnova, whom he had met while working at the printers'.

He publishes his first poem, "Birch," in January 1914. On 21 December, his son Yuri is born.

On 8 March 1915 he leaves Moscow for St. Petersburg (then called Petrograd to disassociate the name with Germany, Russia's enemy in the on-going Great War). The very next day he pays a visit to Alexander Blok, Russia's most famous contemporary poet, subsequently introducing himself to a large number of poets and writers living in the city, including Mayakovsky, Gorky, Akhmatova and her then husband, poet Nikolai Gumilev.

From 1916 he publishes many poems, both individually and in collections every year. He is called to arms on 25 March and on 16 April takes up duty on Sanitary Train No. 143, traveling on it to the front. He reads his poetry to Empress Alexandra on 22 July.

In February 1917 he meets distinguished author and poet Andrei Bely. (In the turmoil of the February Revolution and its wake, Tsar Nicholas II abdicates in March.) On 30 July he marries actress Zinaida Raikh at a Moscow church.

Their daughter Tatyana is born on 29 May 1918. That autumn he befriends Anatoly Marienhof; and on 7 November, to commemorate the revolution, his "Cantata" is performed on Red Square. In December he becomes a member of the Union of Moscow Writers.

In February 1919 the publishing cooperative "Imaginists" is launched. In August he becomes a member of the All-Russian Union of Poets.

His son Konstantin is born on 3 February 1920, and in July he sets out for a trip, reciting his poetry in such cities and towns as Rostov-on-the-Don, Pyatigorsk, Baku and Tbilisi. He meets Galina Benislavskaya on 4 November.

He spends 13 May to 3 June 1921 in Tashkent, where he meets with local writers and recites his poetry, making a side trip to Samarkand. In the autumn he first encounters American dancer Isadora Duncan, and his marriage to Raikh is ended. In December his only play, *Pugachev*, is published.

He marries Duncan on 2 May 1922, eight days later flying with her to Germany. They eventually visit France, Belgium and Italy before leaving Europe for the United States. That autumn collections of his poems are published in Paris, Berlin and Moscow.

He meets with Leon Trotsky at the Kremlin on 3 August 1923. In November he is accused, along with others, of anti-Semitic actions and is arrested; but the following month the court grants permission for him to continue to write and publish. On 17 December he enters a clinic for people with mental illnesses.

He is admitted to Sheremetev Hospital on 13 February 1924, transferring the next month to the Kremlin Hospital. On 12 May his son Alexander is born. In June he meets Anna Akhmatova for the last time. The "Imaginists" is dissolved on 31 August and the dissolution is announced to the press. Four days later he sets out on a trip to the Caucasus, and arrives on 20 September in Baku, where he meets poet Pyotr Chagin.

By 1 March 1925 he has relocated to Moscow, four days later meeting Sophia Tolstaya. He returns to Baku for a visit at the end of March. On 20 May he meets renowned theater director Konstantin Stanislavsky. This year he publishes prolifically in journals and books, becoming, arguably, Russia's most popular poet. On 18 September he marries Tolstaya. On 13 November he finishes "The Man in Black," and on the 26th he is sent to the clinic attached to Moscow State University. On 23 December he leaves Moscow for Leningrad, moving the next day into Room No. 5 at the Hotel Angleterre.

In the middle of the night between 27 and 28 December, 1925, he takes his own life. He is buried at Vagankovsky Cemetery in Moscow on the last day of that year.

Index of Poems

Lightning Source UK Ltd.
Milton Keynes UK
UKHW011857040321
379804UK00001B/65

9 781911 221913